THE TEACHING
DELUSION 3

POWER UP YOUR PEDAGOGY

BRUCE ROBERTSON

First Published 2021

by John Catt Educational Ltd,
15 Riduna Park, Station Road,
Melton, Woodbridge IP12 1QT

Tel: +44 (0) 1394 389850
Email: enquiries@johncatt.com
Website: www.johncatt.com

ISBN: 978 1 913622 70 1

Set and designed by John Catt Educational Limited

PRAISE FOR TTD3: POWER UP YOUR PEDAGOGY

When teachers gather together to reflect on their practice or when individual teachers are self-reflecting or working with a coach, it's so important to have a shared understanding of the problems and solutions under discussion; there needs to be a common framework of some kind. In Power Up Your Pedagogy, *Bruce Robertson has provided teachers with exactly the kind of framework they need. The 12 elements are a superb way of describing the teaching practices we all need to engage with, each supported by an excellent range of Trusted Techniques that are described with crisp clarity; some are reassuringly familiar while others are fresh and innovative. The Power-up Prompts add an excellent layer to the whole process, helping teachers to reflect on their practice as they seek to improve in each area. The range of ideas and references packed into this concise, punchy book is impressive and I can see it doing a superb job of supporting teachers at every career stage.*

Tom Sherrington, author of *The Learning Rainforest*
and *Teaching WalkThrus*

We now have a lot of evidence about how the brain learns but we are less secure about how to use that evidence in the classroom. To my mind, this book is one of the best practical guides a teacher or school leader can have in how to firstly understand and then apply evidence in the classroom.

Dr Carl Hendrick, co-author of *How Learning Happens*

I had the privilege of reading The Teaching Delusion 3: Power Up Your Pedagogy *in the week before returning to school after the summer holidays. As I read, my dusty teacher brain was quickly and forcefully awakened. The joy, knowledge and passion that transmits from every page of this book is impossible not to share. Bruce breaks down a range of complex teaching ideas into simple and easily actionable steps that teachers at every stage of their career would benefit from reflecting on. It is all achieved with huge empathy and humour – Bruce even manages to get the lyrics from the New Radicals into his section on modelling standards ('you get what you give')! It is the most excited I have felt in returning to the classroom for years: armed with numerous 'Power-up Prompts' and 'Trusted Techniques', the young people in my classroom won't know what has hit them. I urge teachers to give this brilliant celebration of our complex craft the time and attention it deserves.*

Jamie Thom, English Teacher and author of *Slow Teaching*

Have you ever been given lesson observation feedback that left you more despondent and frustrated than motivated and energised?' So begins Bruce Robertson's book, The Teaching Delusion 3, and the nodding along begins. Yes, yes, we have, and we certainly don't want more of the same. Robertson's main premise here is, by understanding more about how effective teaching works, mentors, coaches, and leaders can support teachers to improve their practice by giving specific, focused feedback which can have a significant impact on the learning that takes place. Part 1 neatly explores some of the key principles of the science of learning, looking at cognitive load, retrieval practice and schema theory. This is condensed and clear and provides a framework for the next part, which examines how these ideas relate directly to the classroom, with specific examples around areas such as making use of learning intentions and questioning. Each chapter includes prompts to 'power up' your pedagogy and the book provides a breadth of topics covering everything a teacher would need to develop their practice. This book will be invaluable to those who are coaching, particularly building on the Early Careers Framework and Initial Teacher Training. However, I think it will also be found valuable by anyone wanting to reflect on their practice and begin to delve into research to support them to do so.

Zoe Enser, English Adviser for The Education People, specialist adviser for The Teacher Development Trust, and ex English Teacher, Head of Department and Senior Leader

In The Teaching Delusion 3, *Robertson lays the foundations for addressing the issues that arise around poor feedback within the teaching profession. Robertson takes you on a learning journey that is underpinned by research and his own experience to bring together the core principles of effective pedagogy. The Learning Lessons at the beginning underpin how we learn and what follows is a comprehensive toolkit of strategies that every teacher can consider and implement in their own classroom. This is a book that truly will power up your pedagogy!*

Michael Chiles, Associate Assistant Principal
and author of *The Feedback Pendulum*

Being a huge fan of The Teaching Delusion, *I was slightly cynical about whether the follow-up,* The Teaching Delusion 3: Power Up Your Pedagogy, *would live up to its predecessor. In actual fact, Bruce has somehow written something even more practical and relevant for the classroom. I love how well it links to the pedagogical seeds planted in his first book, although it can be read as a stand-alone. Another positive is the ease with which it can be used by teachers as a tool for improvement, both individually and collaboratively as a coaching resource. Bruce's wealth of experience and expertise is reflected in the clearly structured and thought-provoking 'Power-up Prompts', which I could see being excellent discussion points during collegiate conversations. The 'Trusted Techniques' are so useful, showcasing a range of best bets for excellent learning and teaching in the classroom. This is the book I wish I'd had to help me grow as a new teacher, but one which I will return to again and again as a middle leader supporting all teachers in the classroom. When time is precious for all in education, it's important to prioritise professional reading and this would be the first book I would go to, by an experienced and trusted author, for pragmatic, impactful professional learning. A must-read for anyone with an interest in effective learning and teaching.*

Fiona Leadbeater, Principal Teacher of Expressive Arts,
Oban and Tiree High Schools

The Teaching Delusion 3 *is a must-read for any teacher who wants to improve their practice (i.e. all teachers) and also for anyone acting as a coach/mentor to a colleague. The book begins with 10 'Learning Lessons', which summarise how learning happens, with plenty of footnotes for anyone who wants to read more. In the heart of the book, Bruce goes on to go through 12 Elements of pedagogy, and how these can be used to improve learning and teaching in the classroom. Within each Element, there are Power-up Prompts that will make you think about a specific aspect of teaching, and Trusted Techniques, which are specific practices that can be tried in the classroom to improve your practice.*

Bruce has created a fantastic resource that teachers can use to identify aspects of their practice that they'd like to improve, and gives suggested techniques on how these aspects can be improved. Throughout the book there are plenty of concrete examples of how the techniques could be implemented. The book is also ideal for anyone in a coaching or mentoring relationship with a colleague, as it will help the coach/mentor to provide specific, actionable feedback focused on improving classroom practice.

As with his other books, Bruce has written a book that I wish had been written 15 years ago, as I know I would have been a better teacher, mentor and leader if I'd had this book to hand. The Trusted Techniques are mostly strategies that can be implemented very quickly with no huge impact on workload – the sort of professional learning that I like! I'll definitely be recommending it to the student teachers that I work with.

Colin McGill, Lecturer in Education (Chemistry),
Edinburgh Napier University

This book is excellent and a must-have resource for everyone in education, from senior leaders to student teachers. It is a simple and practical guide to support the reader's desire to improve their teaching and learning. Its flexibility allows it to be used both when planning and when reflecting on lessons, either individually or together with colleagues and within faculties or whole-school settings. The simplicity is in the book's format. A concise and well-illustrated chapter on Learning Lessons and how learning takes place allows the reader to fully appreciate the need for each of the 12 key Elements of pedagogy. The practicality of the book is demonstrated by the suggestions of how each Element can be improved using Power-up Prompts, supported by Trusted Techniques (specific practices) which can be used to improve this aspect. *The book then becomes an invaluable reference point to support professional learning, either as a self-help or coaching guide, with exemplars of how this could be used in the short- and long-term professional learning planning process.*

Colin Richardson, Principal Teacher of Teaching & Learning,
Eyemouth High School

As a teacher or a leader, have you ever wished for a 'great teaching' manual? Something that is readable, specific to the classroom and easy to implement in your practice? If you have, then look no further than The Teaching Delusion 3 *– it really is the 'great teaching' manual you have been after!*

As always, Bruce Robertson has engaged in a vast amount of research and simplified this into a powerful and easy read. The Teaching Delusion 3 *considers every detail and provides a refreshing and inspiring take on what great teaching is. As you read and consider the messages of this book, it becomes truly addictive. Bruce's messages are clear, empowering and just make sense – something we have all craved for so long.*

Bruce has carefully crafted this book as a coaching companion for self or peer use. It lends itself perfectly to dip in and out of, or as the perfect text for any professional reading group. I strongly believe that for anyone who teaches or observes teaching, this is a must-read.

Jamie Orr, Teacher, Law Primary School, North Berwick

Power Up Your Pedagogy *is a one-stop shop for classroom, department and school improvement. It is more than useful hints and tips – it's based on extensive research and considerable experience. It's from those two sources that Bruce Robertson is able to hand 'power' to the teacher. I might even dare to say that a teacher could find a career's worth of advice, challenge and support in this book. I wholeheartedly recommend it to teachers in whatever teaching situation they find themselves in.*

Ian Yule, former Principal Teacher of English,
and Principal Teacher of Support for Learning

The Teaching Delusion 3 *is an invaluable resource for teachers looking for research-based, tried-and-tested practical ideas for the classroom, bringing theory and practice together in a very useful way. Its concise way of aligning Power-up Prompts and Trusted Techniques with solid pedagogical principles is the quick-reference guide that every classroom teacher needs. Along with 'TTD1' and 'TTD2', it is the quintessential educational trilogy.*

Derek Huffman, Principal Teacher of Pedagogy,
Berwickshire High School

For Dad

Left to my own devices, I probably would. (Neil Tennant)

Foreword by Kate Jones

This book packs a powerful punch! Bruce Robertson writes with a refreshing and direct honesty combined with wisdom, insight and expertise that comes from years of experience in the classroom. This book finishes off the ultimate teaching and learning trilogy, a collection that will benefit all teachers and school leaders and will therefore benefit students in schools too.

Robertson discusses the poor teaching strategies that have plagued the profession for too long, but this is not done with a judgemental or patronising tone. Instead, it is done with empathy, understanding and a passion to do better through promoting an evidence-informed powerful pedagogy. Discussion of poor and ineffective techniques is important because we can all form bad habits or perhaps are not always aware or do not understand (we can be deluded!) why some of the things we do in the classroom don't have the impact we hoped for.

Reflection is a key theme throughout the book, as the author reflects and encourages the reader to do so too. Robertson acts as a teaching coach, mentor and guide whilst also encouraging the reader to focus on self-improvement and collaboration with colleagues to continually improve and develop.

This book feels like the book that keeps on giving, with words of wisdom and priceless advice on every page. (The suggestions are those I wish I had received throughout my career, especially after lesson observations!) The power-up prompts are applicable and adaptable regardless of the subject or age range taught. There are almost one hundred tried and tested 'trusted techniques' that Robertson generously shares with us to help us all improve our day-to-day classroom practice, which is ultimately what every teacher and school leader wants from a book focused on teaching and learning.

The breadth and depth that Robertson manages to cover in this book is truly remarkable! Cognitive science application in the classroom is explained with clarity and precision, combining in-depth theory and interesting classroom anecdotes. From repetition to retrieval practice, PowerPoint design, feedback, meaningful discussion and much, much more, there are a wealth of practical takeaways for the teacher to implement in their own classrooms to make students think hard.

Teachers and students alike can be full of misconceptions about learning – or as Robertson describes, we are full of delusions. The powered-up planning can dissolve the delusions and help us to prepare powerful lessons and promote long-term learning. The layout and structure of this book supports the reader (as Robertson practises what he preaches by being mindful of cognitive load, the importance of paying attention and crystal-clear communication), meaning this is a book that teachers and leaders at all levels will return to time and time again. It is also a thoroughly enjoyable read.

Robertson provides plenty of food for thought as well as opportunities for the reader to reflect, explore key elements of classroom practice that are often neglected or not discussed as much as they should be, and get to grips with evidence-informed teaching and learning strategies. This book will certainly power up your pedagogy as well as power up your passion to get in the classroom and teach effectively to support the students in front of you as best you can.

Kate Jones

Teacher, leader and author of *Love to Teach: Research and Resources for Every Classroom*, The *Retrieval Practice* series and *Wiliam & Leahy's Five Formative Assessment Strategies in Action*. @Katejones_teach

Contents

Introduction:
Burning Brightly

Have you ever been given lesson observation feedback that left you more despondent and frustrated than motivated and energised? If you have, you are in good company. A process that should be one of *the* most useful to teachers has become the opposite. Rather than welcoming lesson observations with open arms, teachers are locking their doors and turning the lights off. If they manage to get through the year without one, it's a good result!

Not only is this sad, it is deeply damaging to our profession. High-quality feedback offers one of the best ways for teachers to learn and develop their practice. Teachers *need* it! What they don't need is what many are currently getting: **poor-quality feedback** delivered in a **poor-quality way.**

Poor-quality feedback...

At the risk of causing offence to some, too many school leaders are giving lesson observation feedback when they don't really know what they are talking about. I'm sorry, but this needs to be called out. I'm referring to people who sit teachers down and tell them things like:

- You need to talk less.
- You need to differentiate more.
- There was a lack of pace and challenge.
- There wasn't enough group work.
- Students need to be allowed to lead their own learning.

- There wasn't enough higher-order thinking.

Not only are most of these statements too ambiguous to have any real meaning, they are ill-informed. They lack grounding in educational research about high-quality teaching. At best, teachers don't know what to do with them, so they are ignored. At worst, teachers are sent down blind alleys and their teaching actually suffers.

Sometimes, the feedback teachers are given doesn't even relate to *teaching*. For example:

- Your display boards aren't very neat.
- Maybe you could smile a bit more.
- Improve the labelling on your trays.

Such feedback is subjective and ideological. It is based purely on opinion. As a result, it isn't particularly useful to teachers. **Teachers need feedback that is based on *research* and *evidence*.**

...delivered in a poor-quality way
As disappointing as *what* many teachers are being told in feedback is *how* they are being told this. Discussions are rushed. Sometimes, there is no discussion at all. Instead, teachers are sent an email that lists someone's thoughts. Invariably, there is criticism: 'I didn't think you did *that* particularly well'; 'You should have done more of *this*, and much less of *this*'. Sometimes, strategies that are used to give feedback to students, such as 'two stars and a wish', are used with teachers. The fact that this *might* be perceived as patronising appears to go over their heads.

How, precisely, do the people delivering feedback in this way think it is being received? Do they think teachers are grateful? Do they think they are running to the classroom next door to tell their colleague all about it? Do they think they can't wait for their next observed lesson? No? Then why are they delivering feedback like this?

About this book
The Teaching Delusion 3 has been written to help address the significant issue of poor feedback in the teaching profession. It can be used in two ways:

1. By teachers, as a **self-improvement resource**
2. By teachers in collaboration with colleagues, as a **coaching resource**

We will begin with **'A Crash Course in Learning'**, exploring how learning happens via 10 'Learning Lessons'. There are fundamentals here that every teacher and school leader needs to know.

Next, we will get into the real heart of the book: an exploration of *pedagogy*. We will do this by breaking great teaching down into 12 **Elements**, very similar to those first explored in *The Teaching Delusion*:

Element 1. Daily Review

Element 2. Learning Intentions

Element 3. Success Criteria

Element 4. Prior Knowledge

Element 5. Presenting Content

Element 6. Practice

Element 7. Differentiation

Element 8. Questioning

Element 9. Discussion

Element 10. Feedback

Element 11. Plenary Review

Element 12. Expectations, Behaviour & Relationships

As we explore each Element, we will identify associated **Power-up Prompts**. These are summary statements designed to pull together key messages and help you reflect on your teaching practice. There are 75 in total. Don't worry about these just now – they will make sense once we get to them.

We will also identify **Trusted Techniques**. These are specific practices that you can focus on building into your teaching, or on improving further. There are almost 100 in total. Again, these will make sense later.

To finish, we will explore how the key ideas of this book can be brought together in **Professional Learning Plans**, and how these can be used to bring a school together in a culture of learning.

Burning brighter

Teachers have a natural burning desire to keep getting better. To do this, they need access to high-quality professional learning that they can engage in both themselves and with others. This is precisely what this book hopes to provide.

As a self-improvement and coaching resource, it has been written to fuel the professional learning flame, firing everyone up to make their teaching better (no matter how good it is already). Poor lesson observation feedback should be a thing of the past. No longer will it extinguish flames.

Let's get going!

PART 1:
A CRASH COURSE IN LEARNING

A Crash Course in Learning

What is learning and how does it happen? This is a key question for all teachers and school leaders to consider. However, it is also a question that many teachers and school leaders have *never* considered. When you step back and think about it, this really is quite shocking.

Until relatively recently, I was guilty of having never considered this question. As a teacher, I simply taught in the way that I thought was best. This was a blend of how I had been taught at school, what I had learned in teacher training, and tacit learning based on experience. I was doing a good job, but had I known more about learning and how it happens, it would have been significantly better.

Looking back on this, I actually feel quite irritated. It's hard to believe I could have got through teacher training without being taught about learning and how it happens. But I did. It's equally hard to believe that so few people talk about this in schools. But they don't. Mention 'working memory', 'schema' or 'cognitive load' to a random teacher or school leader and wait for the reaction. The safe bet is bemusement. But really, the only bemusing thing is that everyone in schools doesn't know about these things.

I think Craig Barton captures this best:

> A teacher not considering how their students think and learn is kind of like a doctor not being overly concerned about the workings of the body, or a baker taking only a casual interest in the best conditions for bread to rise.[1]

---

1   Barton, C. (2018) *How I Wish I'd Taught Maths*

There are many such doctors and bakers in the teaching profession today. The 'Learning Lessons' that follow are designed to address this.

Learning lessons

Learning Lesson 1: Learning is the development of *long-term memory*, through the accumulation of *knowledge*.

Learning Lesson 2: We *learn* what we *think about*.

Learning Lesson 3: What we *think* depends on what we *know*.

Learning Lesson 4: We are full of *misconceptions*.

Learning Lesson 5: *Cognitive load* controls thinking and learning.

Learning Lesson 6: *Familiarity* and *learning* are not the same thing.

Learning Lesson 7: Over time, *learning fades*.

Learning Lesson 8: *Spaced retrieval* is the best way to prevent forgetting.

Learning Lesson 9: *Overlearning* leads to fluency.

Learning Lesson 10: *Novices* and *experts* think and learn differently.

Learning Lesson 1: Learning is the development of *long-term memory*, through the accumulation of *knowledge*.

Our brains have two memory compartments: **working memory** and **long-term memory**. Working memory is where *thinking* happens; long-term memory is where *storing* happens.[2]

When we take information in from our environment, it enters our working memory first. From there, one of two things can happen:

1. It can 'fall out', meaning we forget it.
2. It can move into our long-term memory, where we store it.

---

2   Willingham, D.T. (2009) *Why Don't Students Like School?*

Information is stored in long-term memory as *knowledge*: knowledge *of things* (declarative knowledge) and knowledge *of how to do things* (procedural knowledge).

The knowledge we have stored in long-term memory can be *retrieved*, meaning it can be brought back into working memory. When that happens, we can think with it, using it to make sense of new information.

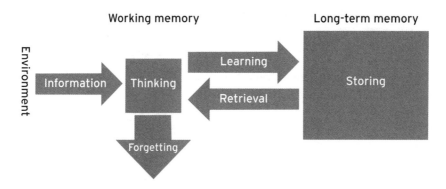

Knowledge is what our working memory *thinks with* and what our long-term memory *stores*. Knowledge is the currency of thinking and learning.

With this in mind, it makes sense to define learning in terms of knowledge. **Learning is the development of *long-term memory*, through the accumulation of *knowledge*.**[3]

This is an extension of the definition proposed by Kirschner et al., which is that learning is 'a change in long-term memory'.[4] You can take your pick as to which you prefer. The most important thing is you understand that learning is all about *long-term memory* and *knowledge*. Teachers are in the long-term memory business.

---

3   Robertson, B. (2020) *The Teaching Delusion*

4   Kirschner, P.A. et al. (2010) 'Why Minimal Guidance During Instruction Does Not Work'

Learning Lesson 2: We learn what we *think about.*

Teaching is concerned with helping students take relevant information in from their **environment** and move this from **working memory** into **long-term memory**. The key to this transfer is *thinking.*

Cognitive scientist Daniel Willingham makes this clear by highlighting that people tend to *learn what they think about.*[5] Educational researchers such as Robert Coe et al. do the same by suggesting that *learning happens when people have to think hard.*[6] The common thread is **thinking**.

To help make this point, Willingham uses the analogy that '**memory is the residue of thought**':[7]

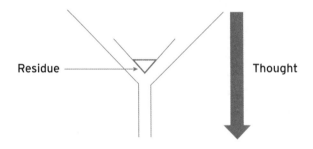

In other words: learning is what is left behind after thinking has taken place.

Paying attention

The first step in getting students to think about something specific is to get them to **pay attention** to it. Nothing can enter long-term memory unless it has first entered working memory. If activities are unstructured or the teacher doesn't take steps to hold students' attention, their minds will wander. They won't be paying attention to what we want them to pay attention to.

---

5   Willingham, D.T. (2009) *Why Don't Students Like School?*
6   Coe, R. et al. (2019) *Great Teaching Toolkit*
7   ibid.

Thinking

The second step is to get students to **think** about what they are paying attention to. Asking them questions and getting them to discuss things tend to be effective ways to do that. However, controlling what, specifically, students are thinking about is one of the great challenges of teaching.

For example, in *The Teaching Delusion*, I discussed a maths lesson in which the teacher related the teaching of fractions to slices of pizza. She did this to help make the lesson interesting and relevant to students' 'real lives'. However, to her dismay, when she quizzed the class about their learning in the next lesson, all students could tell her about was pizza. The *experience of thinking about pizza* was memorable, but *specific learning* about fractions wasn't. Students hadn't been thinking hard enough about this. Therefore, they didn't remember it.

Plan for thinking
Learning is most likely to happen when a *deliberate* attempt is made to *think* about *specific things*. Therefore, when planning and delivering lessons, teachers need to keep asking themselves: what are students likely to be *thinking* about? **Planning for *thinking*** has to be our primary concern. As students engage in activities, it is important that we keep reminding them what it is, *specifically*, that we want them to be thinking about.

Learning Lesson 3: What we *think* depends on what we *know*.

As we have discussed, thinking takes place in **working memory**. In order to be able to think about new information, working memory needs something to think with. What it thinks with is knowledge we have stored in **long-term memory**. The purpose of long-term memory is to *support thinking*.

Schema

The knowledge we have stored in long-term memory doesn't sit in isolation. Rather, it is organised as '**schema**' (or '**schemata**', which is the plural). Schemata are *knowledge constructs*, in which knowledge of particular facts, concepts and procedures are linked to related ones:

Students think with the schemata they have developed and stored in long term memory. When they encounter new information, they pull the relevant schema from long-term memory, into working memory, to help make sense of it. This is why Daniel Willingham suggests that **'understanding is remembering in disguise'**.[8]

For example, imagine you show students the following diagram:

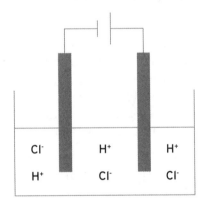

To make sense of this, they need to draw on schemata. **What they see will be determined by what they already know.**[9] If they know that 'Cl⁻' is the chemical symbol for a chloride ion, this is what they will see. If they don't know that, they will see something different, or they might not understand what they are seeing at all.

The same principle applies to what students hear. If you start to talk about 'ions', this will only make sense to students if they have developed

8   Willingham, D.T. (2009) *Why Don't Students Like School?*

9   Kirschner, P.A. and Hendrick, C. (2020) *How Learning Happens*

an 'ions schema'. The more detailed and the better organised this is, the more they will understand about ions, and the more what they are hearing will make sense to them.

Activating schemata

When we think about something, we tend to also think about related things. The reason is because when we **'activate'** a schema by pulling it from long-term memory into working memory, we activate different parts of it, rather than just one part.

For example, if I say 'Richard III', your 'Richard III schema' is activated. You *might* think:

- King
- England
- Shakespeare
- Princes in the tower
- 'A horse! a horse! my kingdom for a horse'.

If you do, it is because these are all a part of your Richard III schema.

You *might* also think:

- Hamlet
- Ian McKellen
- Lord of the Rings

If you do, it is because there are links from your Richard III schema to different schemata, which get activated as a result of your thinking about Richard III.

As Dylan Wiliam points out, **'The purpose of the curriculum is to build up the content of long-term memory so that when students are asked to think, they are able to think in more powerful ways.'**[10] Hence, as teachers, we need to be concerned with how well we are developing students' schemata.

---

10   Wiliam, D. (2018) *Creating the Schools Our Children Need*

Learning Lesson 4: We are full of *misconceptions*.

When students *learn*, they accumulate knowledge in pre-existing schemata. These provide a structure in which new knowledge can be integrated and organised.[11] Knowledge *builds on* and *links to* that which is already stored.

Both helpfully and unhelpfully for teachers, students arrive at our lessons with preformed schemata. Some of what is included in these is 'accurate' knowledge, but some of it isn't. Like you and me, students are full of delusions.

In teaching, we usually refer to delusions as **'misconceptions'**. These are usually the result of students trying to make sense of something when they don't have the prerequisite knowledge to do this.

Misconceptions develop in students from a very early age. As they try to make sense of the world, they act like mini scientists, having internal conversations with themselves: 'I wonder what *that* means...', 'Why did *this* happen?', '*This* must mean *that*'. However, without sufficient knowledge to do this, they arrive unwittingly at the wrong conclusions.

For example, what follows is a list of common misconceptions that students have relating to science:[12]

- Plants grow because they take in food from the soil. *(Plants grow because they use carbon dioxide and water to make sugar (and oxygen) – they can grow without soil.)*
- Putting clothes on something will make it warm. *(Clothes only help to keep something warm because they insulate it – they help to stop heat from escaping.)*
- The heavier an object is, the more likely it is to sink when put into water. *(Whether or not something sinks is determined by its density, not how heavy it is – trees float; 1p coins don't.)*

---

11   Myatt, M. (2018) *The Curriculum*
12   Adapted from: Naylor, S. and Keogh, B. (2000) *Concept Cartoons in Science Education*

- Acids are dangerous. *(Some acids are dangerous, but it depends on both the acid we are talking about and how concentrated it is – the citric acid found in lemons isn't particularly dangerous; nor is the lactic acid you produce in your body during exercise.)*
- When substances dissolve, they go away. *(Some substances look as if they have gone away when they dissolve – such as salt and sugar – but you only have to taste the water to realise that they haven't.)*

Misconceptions are problematic for teachers. Because students use what they already know to make sense of new things, if there is a misconception it is unlikely they can do this. More likely, they will become confused, give up or develop a bigger misconception. As Graham Nuthall tells us: 'No answer is trusted unless it makes logical sense within the context of the child's existing knowledge and beliefs.'[13]

As teachers, an important part of our job is to *uncover misconceptions* and *weed them out*. This means dismantling parts of schema and rebuilding them. In doing so, we need to make it clear to students *why* something is a misconception. If they don't understand that, they are likely to revert back to their misconception further down the line. This is why, in the science examples I have given, I followed each one with an explanation. Had I not done that, if you had this misconception it is less likely it would be corrected.

Learning Lesson 5: *Cognitive load* controls thinking and learning.

As we have discussed, **thinking takes place in working memory**. However, our working memory is limited both in terms of *the space it has to think* and *how long it can hold information*. These limits are the bottleneck of learning.[14]

Cognitive Load Theory[15] explores the limits of working memory and how these can be overcome. Dylan Wiliam has described this as 'the

---

13   Nuthall, G. (2007) *The Hidden Lives of Learners*
14   Lovell, O. (2020) *Sweller's Cognitive Load Theory in Action*
15   Sweller, J. (1988) 'Cognitive Load During Problem Solving'

single most important thing for teachers to know'.[16] If teachers need to know it, then school leaders need to know it too.

What is cognitive load?

Anything that takes up space in our working memory can be thought of as causing **cognitive load**. The *right amount* of the *right type* of load is likely to lead to learning. The *wrong amount* of the *wrong type* will hold learning back. The reason is because our working memory can only cope with a limited amount of load at one time. Once its limit is exceeded, working memory goes into **cognitive overload**, whereby thinking slows down, we stop understanding things, and we make mistakes. If we want students to learn, then we need to ensure there is load, but not too much load, and not the wrong type.[17]

Types of load

There are two types of cognitive load:

1. **Intrinsic load**
2. **Extraneous load**

Effectively, intrinsic load is 'good load' and extraneous load is 'bad load'. That's perhaps oversimplifying things a little, but it helps to reinforce a key point: to maximise student learning, we should be aiming to *optimise* intrinsic load and *minimise* extraneous load.[18]

Optimising intrinsic load

Intrinsic load is the *natural, unavoidable load* caused by thinking about *anything*. It is essential to learning.

Although I have suggested that it is 'good load', as is often the case, we can have too much of a good thing. Too much intrinsic load will lead to cognitive overload. Hence, we are trying to *optimise* it.

---

16   https://impact.chartered.college/article/shibli-cognitive-load-theory-classroom/

17   Barton, C. (2018) *How I Wish I'd Taught Maths*

18   Lovell, O. (2020) *Sweller's Cognitive Load Theory in Action*

Weightlifting

A useful analogy is weightlifting. If we are to build muscle, we *need* weights to feel heavy, but not too heavy. The same is true of intrinsic load. We *need* intrinsic load if we are to learn. If there isn't enough, we are likely to get bored. If there is too much, we get cognitive overload. As we have said, *optimising* intrinsic load is our goal.

Small levels of intrinsic load mean working memory has a lot of free capacity to think. Having space to think is a good thing, but having too much is wasting our potential to learn.

Increasing intrinsic load should lead to more learning. Getting working memory to think hard should be a good thing, so long as it isn't thinking *too hard*.

If we expect our working memory to think about *too much* at one time, or about content that is *too complicated*, we will overload it. As a result, we will stop being able to think, we will make mistakes, and learning will stop.

If we expect our working memory to think about *too much* at one time, or about content that is *too complicated*, we will overload it. As a result, we will stop being able to think, we will make mistakes, and learning will stop.

Complexity of content

The amount of intrinsic load that working memory experiences is related to the *complexity* of content being presented. The more complex content is, the more intrinsic load it is likely to cause. For example, the calculation 346×654 is likely to cause more intrinsic load than 6×12.

The word 'likely' is important. The amount of intrinsic load caused by particular content will vary from student to student, depending on what they know or can do already. In other words, the amount of intrinsic load students experience will depend on **the knowledge they have stored in long-term memory**. Those with *larger, better organised* stores – relevant to the content being thought about – are likely to experience less intrinsic load than those with the opposite.[19]

---

19   Lovell, O. (2020) *Sweller's Cognitive Load Theory in Action*

Accordingly, **ensuring students have secure prerequisite knowledge** *before teaching new content* is essential for teachers if cognitive overload is to be avoided. This can be built on, gradually. As students learn more, they will be able to cope with more.

The importance of background knowledge

Intrinsic load helps explain **why teaching students a *broad, deep body of knowledge* is so important**. If students don't have prerequisite knowledge *stored in long-term memory*, they will have to *look this up* and *hold it in working memory*. As well as making the learning process laborious and slow,[20] this causes avoidable intrinsic load. **This load could be avoided if the knowledge students needed was stored in their long-term memory.** Here, it could be accessed quickly, as and when required. The space now available in working memory could be used for thinking, rather than for temporary storage.

Just as building muscle allows us to lift heavier weights, developing long-term memory allows students to think about more complex things.

Break it down

Excessive intrinsic load can also be avoided if **complex content is broken down and presented in smaller, cumulative chunks**. The natural intrinsic load of the content is still there, but this is processed gradually, rather than all at once. Long-term memory can be used to store each chunk, giving working memory access to it, when required. Once learned, one by one the chunks can be brought together and processed in working memory. *Now* students are able to *think about the full complexity of the content*, but the load is reduced. Long-term memory is helping working memory out.

Minimising extraneous load

Extraneous load is the *unnecessary, avoidable load* associated with **how content is presented**. Because it doesn't lead to learning, it can be thought of as 'bad load'. We aren't trying to 'optimise' extraneous load; we are trying to *minimise* it.

---

20   Barton, C. (2018) *How I Wish I'd Taught Maths*

Extraneous load tends to be caused when students are expected to **pay attention to too much at once**. Quite simply, there is too much information coming at them. For example:

- Our slides are crammed with text, much of which is unnecessary.
- Our slides are crammed with clipart.
- Our explanations are too wordy and long-winded.
- There is too much noise in the room.
- Students have to look at multiple sources of information at one time in order to understand what is being presented.

Because all of these things cause extraneous load, none of them are good for learning. The more extraneous load there is, the less intrinsic load working memory can process. Hence, the less it can think about the things that are most important for it to be thinking about.

Careful instructional design is the key to minimising extraneous load and freeing up as much working memory as possible for thinking.

Learning Lesson 6: *Familiarity* and *learning* are not the same thing.

Sometimes we think we know or understand something when, actually, we don't. We only find this out when we have been tested in some way. **Familiarity can lead to overconfidence.**[21]

I have found this to be true in all walks of life. For example, when I am watching the US television series *Homeland* with my husband, he says to me, 'Do you understand what's happening?', and I say, 'Yes'. And then I try to explain what's happening, and I realise that I can't. Being asked a question about it has highlighted that I only have a *loose, superficial* understanding of something that I thought I had a deeper understanding of but didn't.

---

21   Bjork, E.L. and Bjork, R.A. (2014) 'Making Things Hard on Yourself, But in a Good Way'

Check, check, check

For learning in schools, this helps explain why **it isn't enough to *cover* content. We need to *check* that content is being *learned*.** Our teaching needs to be about both *schema building* and *schema checking*. To do this, we need to make the content of students' long-term memory visible.

Visible learning

The best way to make students' learning visible is to ask them questions. By listening carefully to what they say, we can find out how much they know and understand.

Even better is if we can get students to articulate knowledge and understanding in *writing* or in *drawings*. Now, the content of long-term memory is *really* visible. Use of **Show-me boards** is an excellent way to do this. Show-me boards help to make *everyone's* learning visible to the teacher.

Learning Lesson 7: Over time, *learning fades.*

When we teach students, there is often an 'illusion of learning'. They seem to understand what we are teaching them, and when we assess this at the end of the lesson, we get evidence that they do. However, when they come to the next lesson two days later and we ask them about what they had learned: tumbleweed. How can this be?

The reason is that, over time, *learning fades.* Although information *was* successfully transferred from working memory into long-term memory in the last lesson, it has started to disappear. What we saw in the last lesson was *short-term performance* based on **short-term learning.** *Longer-term performance* requires **longer-term learning.**

Both short-term and longer-term learning involve changes in long-term memory. However, with longer-term learning, the changes are more secure. Developing this security **takes time.** Fading *will* happen. Teachers and students need to accept this and take steps to address it.

Learning Lesson 8: *Spaced retrieval* is the best way to prevent forgetting.

When learning has faded to the point that it can't be retrieved from long-term memory, it is 'forgotten'. As teachers, we need to stop this happening with learning that relates to the curriculum. The key is to ensure there are **regular opportunities for students to *revisit content*.**

The Ebbinghaus Forgetting Curve

The importance of revisiting content is captured by the **Ebbinghaus Forgetting Curve:**[22]

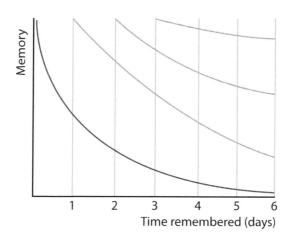

The curve illustrates three important principles of fading and revisiting:

1. When we first learn something, fading is fast (this is captured by the steepness of the first curve).
2. Revisiting content reverses fading.
3. The more content is revisited, the less quickly fading happens.

---

22   https://www.psychestudy.com/cognitive/memory/ebbinghaus-forgetting-curve

The rule of three

Graham Nuthall has suggested that content needs to be revisited on **at least three separate occasions** to mitigate against natural fading.[23] In other words, *as a minimum*:

- *Teach* content.
- Allow some time to pass.
- *Revisit* this content.
- Allow some more time to pass.
- *Revisit* this again.

Learning Lag

The spaced nature of the revisits is important. It creates a **'learning lag'** that is helpful.[24] By allowing learning to fade *a little* and then revisiting it, it can be given a 'jump start', strengthening memory.

For example, you might teach content in a lesson, allow some time to pass, and then revisit this at the end of the lesson. You might also revisit it again at the start of the next lesson, and towards the end of the week. So long as it isn't too long, the lag will benefit learning. The more revisiting, the better.

Types of revisiting

In general, there are two types of revisiting: *passive* and *active*.

Passive revisiting

Passive revisiting occurs when students *see or hear* the same material again. For example, having taught that the part of the brain responsible for coordinating voluntary movements is the cerebellum, the teacher repeats this in a subsequent lesson. Another example would be students reading the same information over and over in their notes. These are passive revisiting activities because students **don't have to *think* about the content being revisited**. While there will be *some* value to learning, this won't be as much as when revisiting is *active*.

---

23   Nuthall, G. (2007) *The Hidden Lives of Learners*

24   'Lag' is discussed in this way in: Hendrick, C. and Macpherson, R. (2017) *What Does This Look Like in the Classroom?*

Active revisiting

Active revisiting occurs when students **have to *think* about the same content again.** If this involves *retrieving knowledge from long-term memory*, then it will utilise **the *Testing Effect*,** which tells us that **recall strengthens memory.**[25]

For example, rather than the teacher reminding students that the part of the brain responsible for coordinating voluntary movements is the cerebellum, students might be asked a question that makes them *recall this* themselves. Rather than students reading notes over and over, they could try to write a summary of everything they know about particular content *from memory.* The effort required to pull information from long-term memory strengthens the memory of it.

The Forgetting Pit

A useful analogy to help understand fading and its relationship to learning is to think of long-term memory as a **'Forgetting Pit':**[26]

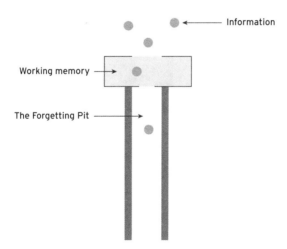

All of the information that enters working memory falls into this pit. *Most* of this is then forgotten, but not everything. *Some* information can

---

25   Barton, C. (2018) *How I Wish I'd Taught Maths*

26   Adapted from: https://theteachingdelusion.com/2020/03/30/the-forgetting-pit/

be brought back out of the pit and thought about. This is information that has been *learned*.

The fact that most information is forgotten is a good thing – nobody needs or wants to remember everything they pay attention to. In teaching, however, forgetting can be frustrating. Teachers need to understand how the Forgetting Pit works to understand how they can best help students learn what they want them to learn.

The Point of No Return
Information can be said to be 'forgotten' if it can't be brought back out of the Forgetting Pit, into working memory, despite prompts and reminders. This happens when *it has fallen too far down the pit to be retrieved*. It has gone past the **Point of No Return:**

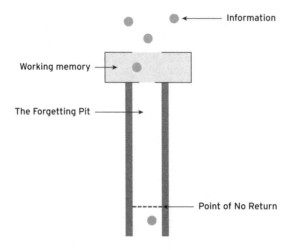

Most of the information we pay attention to falls past this point. However, not all of it does.

Sticky information
Some of the information we pay attention to sticks to the walls of the Forgetting Pit. *This is learning.* **The better information sticks to the wall, the better it is learned.** Information that has been learned – that is, stuck to the wall – can be retrieved:

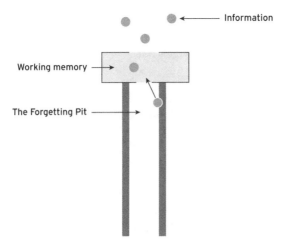

How easily information can be retrieved depends on how far down the pit it has fallen. **The further down the pit something is, the more difficult it is to retrieve:**

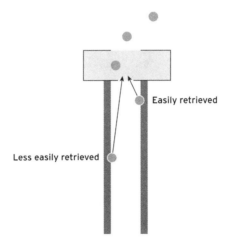

The tendency to forget

Being stuck to the walls of the pit doesn't stop information being forgotten – it can slide down. The rate of sliding isn't the same for everything, and some information isn't sliding at all, but a lot is. What this means is that, over time, a lot of information becomes more difficult to retrieve. As we have said, **Short-term learning** is not the same as **long-term learning**. Eventually, many things that were once easy to retrieve have slid past the Point of No Return and are forgotten.

The rate of forgetting

How quickly information slides down the Forgetting Pit depends on various factors, including *how tightly* stuck to the wall it is and whether or not it *sticks to a schema* already there:

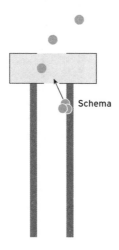

Information that sticks to a pre-existing schema won't slide as quickly down the pit.

Making information 'sticky'

How tightly information sticks to the walls of the pit depends on how 'sticky' it is. As teachers, we should be aiming to make the content of our curriculum as sticky as possible. We do this by giving information a 'sticky coating'.

Some information has this coating already and will stick to the walls of the Forgetting Pit naturally. However, most of it doesn't. Even if it does, the coating usually isn't sticky enough to prevent information eventually sliding past the Point of No Return. It needs to be made *stickier*.

Information can be made stickier when it is thought about in working memory. This is where it gets its sticky coating. The more information is *thought about*, the stickier the coating becomes.

The 'Easily Retrieved Area'

The area of the Forgetting Pit we are aiming to get information to stick to and stay at is the **'Easily Retrieved Area'**:

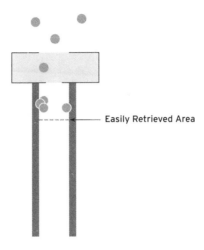

This is the area from which students can retrieve things quickly, as and when they need to. This is the area that is concerned with *long-term* learning. Active revisiting is the key to achieving this.

Learning Lesson 9: *Overlearning* leads to fluency.

Overlearning

Through repeated revisits, preferably actively, we aim for students to **overlearn**.[27] Rather than being *familiar* with content, they have a *secure grasp* of it. They don't just know something – they know it *very well*. They don't just understand something – they have a *deep understanding* of it. The long-term memory is *strong*:

---

27   https://www.psychestudy.com/cognitive/memory/ebbinghaus-forgetting-curve

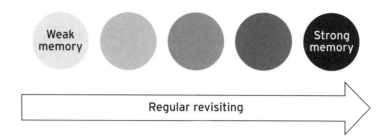

In our analogy of long-term memory as a Forgetting Pit, overlearning results in information being tightly stuck to the walls in the Easily Retrieved Area.

Fluency

Overlearning leads to **fluency**.[28] When students perform fluently, they don't have to think about what they are doing: it is effectively automatic. As a result, they can *think faster* and *think about more*. They are also *less likely to make mistakes*. In our teaching, we should be aiming for *fluent learning*.

Mix revisits up

The one caveat we need to put on this relates to motivation.[29] Whilst fluency should be our goal, we don't want to bore students in the pursuit of this. Repeated revisits risk doing that.

To avoid bored, demotivated students, we need to 'mix revisits up', so each encounter looks different. For example:

Content to be learned	Encounter 1	Encounter 2	Encounter 3
Acids are solutions with a pH of less than 7	Interactive teacher presentation	Closed-book quiz at the start of the next lesson	Completing a short piece of writing, from memory, with the title: 'Everything I know about acids'

---

28   McCourt, M. (2019) *Teaching for Mastery*

29   Willingham, D.T. (2009) *Why Don't Students Like School?*

In *The Teaching Delusion 2*, I discussed this as coming at content from 'different angles'.[30]

Learning Lesson 10: *Novices* and *experts* think and learn differently.

As they overlearn and develop fluency, students move from being 'novices' to 'experts' in particular knowledge domains.

The difference between novices and experts

The difference between novices and experts is in terms of the **schemata** they have. *Experts* in a particular domain have *detailed, organised schemata* in that domain. The schemata of *novices* lack the detail and organisation of experts. Because schemata are what we think and learn with, novices and experts think and learn differently.[31]

Surface structure vs deep structure

An example of this is in the way that novices and experts tackle problems. Novices don't tend to be able to see past the 'surface structure' of problems, which prevents them getting to the 'deep structure' needed to solve it.[32] They get tangled up in superfluous detail and become cognitively overloaded before getting to the root of the problem.

Take the following chemistry problem as an example:[33]

Tennessine is a newly discovered element with a predicted electron arrangement of 2, 8, 18, 32, 32, 18, 7.

In which group of the periodic table should Tennessine be placed?

A. 1

B. 2

C. 7

D. 8

30   Robertson, B. (2021) *The Teaching Delusion 2*

31   https://learningspy.co.uk/learning/novice-expert-model-learning/

32   Kirschner, P.A. and Hendrick, C. (2020) *How Learning Happens*

33   https://www.sqa.org.uk/pastpapers/papers/papers/2019/N5_Chemistry_all_2019.pdf

An expert recognises, almost instantly, that the answer is C. They realise that this is a problem about electron arrangements and groups in the periodic table, and they filter out everything else. They know that *the last number* in an electron arrangement sequence like this tells you which group an element is in. A novice doesn't think like that.

A novice will see the word 'Tennessine' and think: 'I've never heard of that before! My teacher hasn't taught me anything about Tennessine! I don't know how to solve this.'

Even if they get past this, if they don't know that it is the last number in the sequence that's key, they will probably start to think about *all of the numbers*. This will take up a lot of space in working memory. Their internal conversation with themselves goes along the lines: 'What do these numbers mean?' 'I'm not sure.' 'Is it the first number that's important?' 'I don't think so.' 'Is it the biggest number?' 'It could be.' 'Do I need to add or subtract numbers?' 'I can't remember.' Very quickly, their working memory becomes overloaded.

Experts avoid all of this because *relevant knowledge* from *detailed schemata* is recalled *automatically*. This requires almost no effort. The complexity of schemata and the automation of knowledge are what make an expert such.

The Expertise Reversal Effect

Most students are novices in most of the domains they encounter in most subjects. Lacking the detailed schemata necessary for internal 'making sense' conversations, they rely on feedback from external experts.[34] In schools, these external experts are *teachers*.

For novices, **teacher-led approaches** – a blend of *direct-interactive instruction* and *formative assessment* – are almost always better than facilitated approaches when it comes to learning anything new. Novices shouldn't be left to work things out for themselves. As their schemata develop and they become more expert through repeated revisits, the need for a teacher becomes less. At this stage, **student-led approaches** *can* benefit learning. This is known as the ***Expertise Reversal Effect***.[35]

---

34   Willingham, D.T. (2009) *Why Don't Students Like School?*

35   Barton, C. (2018) *How I Wish I'd Taught Maths*

The crucial point is: **Don't leave novices to learn as if they were experts.** They won't learn *as much or as fast* as they could. We will hold learning back.

In Part 1, we have drawn on key principles from cognitive science and educational research to identify 10 Learning Lessons. These are essential for all teachers and school leaders to know.

In Part 2, we shall draw on these as we turn our attention to **Powered-up Pedagogy**.

PART 2: POWERED-UP PEDAGOGY

Introduction to Powered-up Pedagogy

In this section, we are going to explore *pedagogy* in detail. In doing so, we are going to talk about three areas:

1. **Elements**
2. **Power-up Prompts**
3. **Trusted Techniques**

Elements

Pedagogy can be thought about as 12 discrete but related **Elements**. These are:[36]

Element 1. Daily Review

Element 2. Learning Intentions

Element 3. Success Criteria

Element 4. Prior Knowledge

Element 5. Presenting Content

Element 6. Practice

Element 7. Differentiation

---

36 With two exceptions, these mirror the 12 Elements set out in *The Teaching Delusion*. The exceptions relate to *success criteria*, which have been separated from *learning intentions*, and to *relationships*, which have been combined with *expectations and behaviour*.

Element 8. Questioning

Element 9. Discussion

Element 10. Feedback

Element 11. Plenary Review

Element 12. Expectations, Behaviour & Relationships

This section of the book is broken down into chapters that focus on each element.

Power-up Prompts

As we explore each element, we will identify associated **Power-up Prompts**. These are *summary statements* designed to make you *stop and think* about specific aspects of your teaching. There are 75 of them. They have been numbered, for ease of reference.

For example, in our exploration of 'Element 1. Daily Review', the first Power-up Prompt is:

> **Power-up Prompt 1:** Lessons begin with a *review activity*, requiring *recall from long-term memory.*

Power-up Prompts are brought together in a summary at the end of each chapter.

Self-coaching

You can use Power-up Prompts to help **plan lessons**, or to **support your reflection on lessons** after they have been taught. For example, in planning a lesson, you might refer to a Power-up Prompt and ask yourself:

- Have I planned for this to happen?
- How can I plan for this to happen better than it has in the past?

In reflecting on a lesson, you might refer to a Power-up Prompt and ask yourself:

- To what extent do I think this was the case?

- Are there any ways I think this could have been improved?

In this way, Power-up Prompts support **self-coaching**.

Peer coaching

If you are discussing your teaching with someone else, or if they are discussing their teaching with you, Power-up Prompts can help guide the conversation. Instead of talking about random things that may or may not be worth talking about, Power-up Prompts provide focus to the conversation, helping to ensure you are talking about *the right things*.

In this way, Power-up Prompts support **peer coaching**.

Trusted Techniques

Having reflected on specific aspects of your teaching using Power-up Prompts, you may want ideas about how you can develop these. This is where **Trusted Techniques** come in.

Trusted Techniques are *specific practices* you can focus on building into your teaching, or on improving further. There are almost 100 in total. Each one has been given a *name* and *code*, for ease of reference. For example:

- **Last Lesson (TT1)**
- **Empty Your Brain (TT2)**
- **Teacher-quizzing (TT3)**

Like Power-up Prompts, Trusted Techniques are brought together in a summary at the end of each chapter.

Don't worry if all of this doesn't make complete sense just now. There is a lot of terminology that is difficult to get your head around without context. The cognitive load is high. Trust me that this will ease once we get into our exploration.

Let's do that now.

Element 1:
Daily Review

Many schools insist that lessons begin with a 'starter'. However, including a starter for the sake of it is rather pointless. Pointless starters are **'non-gain starters'**[37] – neither students nor the teacher gain anything from them. They are included with the sole purpose of keeping students busy as others arrive, settling the class, or beginning the lesson with something 'fun'. Typically, they take the form of puzzles or games. Often, there is a *loose link* to learning, but this just disguises their non-gain nature. For example:

- in a history lesson, putting a selection of dates in chronological order
- in a music lesson, finding the names of different instruments in a word search
- in a science lesson, solving anagrams relating to key terminology.

Students are quick to see through such starters and devalue them. Rather than rushing to class to get started, they are more likely to take their time, thinking: 'It's just the starter – I won't be missing much.'

This is not how we want students to be thinking. We want them to see the start of a lesson as an essential part of it. Accordingly, we need to plan starter activities as carefully as we do any other part of a lesson.

---

37   McCourt, M. (2019) *Teaching for Mastery*

'Learning gain starters'

'Learning gain starters' are starters that support student and teacher learning. Rather than filling time, they add value. Typically, they are concerned with **reviewing specific prior learning**.

Their value to students comes from *knowledge recall*. Using them will:

1. Strengthen memory (this is *the Testing Effect* in action).[38]
2. Help students to recognise what they know and don't know (or can and can't do).
3. Motivate students to study.[39]

Their value to teachers comes from the information they get from this, which they can *respond to* in this lesson or a future lesson.

Because 'learning gain starters' are typically concerned with *review*, the term **'Daily Review'**[40] is better than 'starter'. It helps to get away from the association with 'being busy activities' that add little value.[41]

> **Power-up Prompt 1:** Lessons begin with a *review activity*, requiring *recall from long-term memory*.

Types of review

Daily Review can take many forms, some open and some more structured. We shall explore a selection of these.

Open review

A simple but effective Daily Review activity is **Last Lesson (TT1)**, whereby students are asked to think about the question: 'What did we learn last lesson?' Framing this as 'learn', as opposed to 'do', is important, because it is learning that we want students to focus on.

---

38   We discussed memory in Learning Lesson 8 in Part 1.

39   Enser, M. (2019) in *The researchED Guide to Education Myths*

40   Rosenshine, B. (2012) 'Principles of Instruction'

41   'Being busy activities' were discussed in Robertson, B. (2021) *The Teaching Delusion 2*. These are activities that engage students, but don't require them to *think hard* about specific content. Hence, they don't typically lead to learning.

Alternatively, students could be asked to **Empty Your Brain (TT2)**, writing down everything that they remember about particular content.

Structured review

Rather than using 'open activities' of the type we have discussed, there is often value in teachers guiding student thinking in a more structured way. **Teacher-quizzing (TT3)** tends to be an effective way to do this.

Teacher-quizzing

In teacher-quizzing, questions can be a variety of types. These include:

- short answer response
- fill in the blanks
- true or false
- odd one out
- deliberate mistakes
- multiple choice.

To make the most of quizzing, teachers need to know what students have previously been taught. Where a curriculum is vague, Daily Review becomes tokenistic and nebulous. Teachers who have a full overview of the curriculum for their discipline, including what has been taught previously and what will be taught in future, are able to make more effective use of Daily Review than those who don't.[42]

For example, quizzing could be used to review content taught several months or years ago. Rather than asking, 'What do you know about the Romans?', the teacher can ask *specific* questions about *specific* content that students should already know.

Show-me Boards

Students can write the answers to teacher quiz questions in their jotter or on **Show-me Boards (TT4)**.

The advantage of the latter is that they allow teachers to check the learning of *all students*, in real time. Answers in jotters tend to remain hidden from view.

---

42   Myatt, M. (2018) *The Curriculum*

Self-quizzing

Rather than the teacher setting the quiz for the class, there can be value in students **Self-quizzing (TT5)**. For example, students could be asked to use the first few minutes of a lesson to test themselves using flash cards, or engaging in a 'read, cover, write, check, correct' activity, using their Knowledge Organiser.[43]

Peer-quizzing

Similarly, **Peer-quizzing (TT6)** can be a powerful Daily Review activity. For example, students could use flash cards to test each other, or their Knowledge Organisers to ask each other questions as the teacher would have in a teacher-led quiz.

Recent and less recent material

Daily Review is often best when it includes a mix of recent and less recent material. As we have previously discussed, by getting students to revisit material from some time ago, we strengthen their memory of this.

For example, if there are five questions in a quiz, three of these might relate to the previous lesson, one to a lesson from last week, and one to a lesson from longer ago. I once observed a teacher who used a template to help them do this as a matter of routine:

Last lesson	Last week	Last month
Question 1 Question 2 Question 3	Question 4	Question 5

Power-up Prompt 2: There is an appropriate blend of *recent and less recent material.*

Daily Review in practice

Like every aspect of our teaching, *planning* Daily Review is important, but more important is the *delivery*. When I observe lessons, I often see

---

43 A Knowledge Organiser is usually one side of A4 which details the *specific knowledge*, including vocabulary, that students need to learn in a topic.

Daily Review that has been well planned but is poorly delivered. To explore this, we will consider two scenarios.

Scenario 1

Imagine you have taught a lesson on electric current. In this, students were supposed to learn what electric current is and how it can be measured. They all have a Knowledge Organiser that summarises this.

You start the next lesson with a Daily Review activity focusing on the learning from the last lesson. Projected onto the screen is a slide that reads: 'Write down everything you know about electric current.' You tell the class that they have two minutes to complete the activity, and that they can look back at their Knowledge Organiser if they need to. You don't give any instruction as to whether or not students can talk. What happens?

Most students look at their Knowledge Organiser and copy information from this. Some chat to the person sitting next to them, but not about electric current. After two minutes, most students have written something, but they haven't finished. A few students haven't written anything. Recognising this, you say (quite loudly, because some students are talking): 'Okay, I'll give you another few minutes to complete this.' A further three minutes pass before you stop the activity. You ask, 'Who can tell me something about electric current?', choosing a few students to answer. Each of them reads something they have written, most of which was copied from their Knowledge Organiser. Satisfied the activity is complete, you move on.

Thinking critically about this scenario should help you to recognise the features of effective – and less effective – Daily Review. For example, ask yourself:

1. Should students have been expected to retrieve information from memory, or was it better that they were allowed to look back at their Knowledge Organiser?

2. Should students have been expected to complete the task in silence, or was it better that they were allowed to talk?

3. Should the teacher have extended the time available, or should they have stuck to the limit they had set?

In answering the first question, if you accept that Daily Review should be about *recall from long-term memory*, then students shouldn't have been allowed to look back at their Knowledge Organiser. By allowing them to do so, you are not testing what they know – you are testing their ability to look something up. It is true that by looking it up, the information is being brought to their attention again, but not in a way that really helps to make it memorable. For their learning, it would be far better if they had to *think hard* and search their long-term memory for the information. At worst, they won't find it, or they will get it wrong. But there's nothing wrong with that – not knowing and getting things wrong are important features of the learning process. Knowing what we don't know empowers us to do something about that. Not knowing what we don't know disempowers us.

The answer to the second question is less clear-cut. There are arguments for and against each option. For example, if you get students to complete this activity in silence, it is less likely that they will go off task. However, if they get stuck, they won't have anyone to spark ideas off or to get help from. But perhaps that isn't the purpose of this task. Perhaps this task is about *individual* learning, not learning together. Whichever it is needs to be clear, both in the teacher's mind and to students. The most important thing is that all students are engaged and thinking about what they are meant to be thinking about. The best bet would probably be to mix it up and use different approaches in different lessons.

> **Power-up Prompt 3:** *All students* are engaged, thinking about what they should be thinking about.

The answer to the third question is also less clear-cut. As with most things, there is a balance to be struck. Every minute spent on Daily Review is a minute that can't be spent on something else. Some people use this as an argument against the use of Daily Review, arguing: 'There's too much content to get through!' However, such arguments miss a fundamental point: **teaching isn't about 'getting through content' – it is about *students learning this content*.**

As discussed in *The Teaching Delusion* and *The Teaching Delusion 2*, most of what we teach isn't learned, certainly not initially.[44] Therefore, it is essential that time is made available *in class* for students to recall learning, so that both they and their teacher can check the size of the **teaching–learning gap**,[45] and respond to this. It is naive to think that all students are going to check and correct their learning in their own time. Some will, but many won't.

Some teachers argue: 'I've done my part – teaching it – now students have to do their part – learning it.' This holds water if you believe a teacher's job is to 'teach', as is implicit in the job title. But if you believe that a teacher's job is to get students to *learn* – all students, learning everything you plan for them to learn – then this argument isn't watertight at all.

So, let's get away from arguments that we don't have time for Daily Review and instead accept that, in the interests of high-quality teaching and learning, we *need* to make proportionate time for it.

Power-up Prompt 4: *A proportionate amount of time* is used for review activities.

Scenario 2

Imagine you start a lesson with a PowerPoint slide that has four tasks on it:

1. Write the definition of an enzyme.
2. True or false: catalysts are enzymes.
3. Name two enzymes found in the human body.
4. Sketch a graph to show the effect of temperature on the activity of an enzyme.

Students are given four minutes to complete this as a closed-book activity, in silence. After four minutes, you go through the answers. You do this

---

44   Robertson, B. (2020) *The Teaching Delusion*; Robertson, B. (2021) *The Teaching Delusion 2*

45   ibid.

interactively, asking students questions and checking for understanding. This takes four minutes. Students correct their own work. You move on to the next part of the lesson.

Ask yourself:

1. Was this effective use of Daily Review?
2. Could anything have happened differently that would have made it *more* effective?

For me, the answer to both questions is 'yes'.

Thought of in light of the Power-up Prompts we have identified to this point, the review activity *was* effective. However, there are *perhaps* other things that could have happened to make it even more so. I stress 'perhaps', because it's not as straightforward as saying: '*This* would definitely have made Daily Review better.' The list of things that we could do to make any aspect of our teaching better is endless, but that doesn't mean we can do all of these things. We only have a finite amount of time available to us. So, as we explore things that *could* be done to make this example of Daily Review better, I ask you to keep this point in mind.

Students *could* have been asked to *total their score* and *record this* in a **Student Review Record (TT7)**. By doing so after each review, they can *track* and *take ownership* of their learning. Such a record should help to direct the focus of self-study.

> **Power-up Prompt 5:** Activities provide *formative information to students.*

There *might* have been value in the teacher finding out how students got on with each question, at both an individual and a class level. For example, they could have asked for a show of hands – 'Who got that one right?' – after going over the answer to each question. This would have given them useful formative information about the teaching–learning gap for the class as a whole.

The teacher *could* have taken a different approach to the activity. Rather than projecting the four questions up at once and giving students time to write answers to these in their jotters, the teacher could have projected the questions up *one at a time* and asked students to write each answer on a Show-me board. The checking and correcting could have taken place after each question, with students keeping score of how they got on. At the end of this, students could have totalled their score and made a record of it. By approaching Daily Review in this way, the teacher maximises the amount of formative information coming to them.

> **Power-up Prompt 6:** Activities provide *formative information to the teacher.*

Weekly & Monthly Review

All of the teaching and learning gains achieved in Daily Review can also be achieved in **Weekly Review** and **Monthly Review**. The key differences between these is the *breadth of content covered* and the *amount of lesson time* they take.

Daily Review	Weekly Review	Monthly Review
Increasing breadth of content, increasing amount of lesson time		

Whenever 'review' takes the form of a quiz, it lends itself to scores being recorded by students and/or the teacher. Whilst I wouldn't advise any teacher to start keeping track of students' scores in Daily Review or Weekly Review (students can do this themselves), I definitely think there is value in teachers keeping track of students' performance in Monthly Review. You would do this by maintaining a **Teacher Review Record (TT8)**.

Such records can be shared with parents, which can help to report student progress. I would argue strongly that these have far more value than the comments many teachers are expected to spend inordinate amounts of time writing in reports.

As with Daily Review, both Weekly Review and Monthly Review can be completed and gone over with students in lessons – teachers don't need to take away extra marking.

> **Power-up Prompt 7:** *Weekly and Monthly Review* are used to complement Daily Review.

Summary

Element 1: Daily Review	
Power-up Prompts	**Trusted Techniques**
1 Lessons begin with a *review activity, requiring recall from long-term memory.*	Last Lesson (TT1) Empty Your Brain (TT2) Teacher-quizzing (TT3) Show-me Boards (TT4) Self-quizzing (TT5) Peer-quizzing (TT6)
2 There is an appropriate blend of *recent and less recent material.*	
3 *All students* are engaged, thinking about what they should be thinking about.	
4 *A proportionate amount of time* is used for review activities.	
5 Activities provide *formative information to students.*	Student Review Record (TT7)
6 Activities provide *formative information to the teacher.*	Teacher Review Record (TT8)
7 *Weekly Review and Monthly Review* are used to complement Daily Review.	

Element 2: Learning Intentions

Not all teachers and school leaders agree that use of learning intentions is important. However, I think this has more to do with *poor approaches* to their use, rather than the principles underpinning them.

The principles underpinning the use of learning intentions are that students need to know:

1. What they are learning
2. If they have learned what they are supposed to have learned.

It's really no more complicated than that. I doubt many teachers or school leaders are against these principles. Rather, it is the way some people have suggested they should be put into practice that they have the problem with. They are right to call that out. Poor practice in relation to learning intentions wastes time and confuses both students and teachers. Unfortunately, there is quite a lot of it.

What are learning intentions?

Learning intentions are statements that summarise the purpose of a lesson in terms of *learning*. A useful acronym is **WALT (TT1)** – 'We Are Learning Today':[46]

- **'We are learning about…'**
- **'We are learning to…'**

---

46   Clarke, S. (2014) *Outstanding Formative Assessment*

In writing them, it is often helpful to use **'Know…'**, **'Understand…'** or **'Be Able to…'** (**TT2**), which helps communicate that the learning will relate to knowledge, understanding or skills, respectively.

Examples:

- We are learning about the structure of an atom, specifically to *know about*:
  – The sub-atomic particles that make up atoms
- We are learning to separate mixtures, specifically to *be able to*:
  – Separate an insoluble substance from water.

Learning intentions should be about what students are *learning*, not what they are *doing*. To appreciate this, consider the following statements:

1. Complete the experiment that we started in the previous lesson.
2. Answer all of the questions on page 60.
3. Take part in a group activity to investigate factors that affect dissolving.

These statements are not learning intentions. They do not fit the definition. Instead, these relate to what students will be *doing* in the lesson. It can be useful for this to be made clear to students, but this isn't the same as sharing a *learning intention* with them.

Power-up Prompt 1: The learning intention relates to *specific learning, not doing.*

Pique interest

Sometimes, rather than word learning intentions as the statements we have just explored, there can be value in wording them as questions. In doing so, we **Pique Interest** (**TT3**).

For example, rather than a learning intention that reads…

- We are learning to separate mixtures, specifically to *be able to*:
  – Separate an insoluble substance from water

…instead, it could read:

- How can we separate an insoluble substance from water?

A reason for doing this would be to help to pique interest, which questions tend to do naturally.[47] As Tom Sherrington reminds us, the more we inspire and interest students in our subjects, the more likely it is that they will want to learn.[48] Depending on what we are teaching, framing a learning intention as a question might be a better way to communicate the learning intended in a lesson than framing it in a statement.

Blending questions and statements

Sometimes, framing learning intentions as questions *and* as statements can complement each other. You might decide to have an overarching learning intention *question* for *a series of lessons*, to which you keep returning, in addition to specific learning intention *statements* for *specific lessons*.

For example, your overarching question might be:

- How can we separate substances that are mixed together?

Specific learning intention statements for specific lessons might be:

- Know how to separate an insoluble substance from water.
- Know how to separate a soluble substance from water.
- Know how a mixture of two liquids can be separated.

Clear communication

Usually, there is value in sharing the learning intention with students *towards the start* of a lesson and revisiting it *towards the end*. This helps to 'frame' the lesson. At the start: 'Today, *this* is our focus.' At the end: 'Remember, we were focusing on *this*.'

How you share it

How you share learning intentions matters. Contrast the teacher who has a pre-written learning intention as part of a PowerPoint presentation with the teacher scribbling one onto a spare piece of board, as if they've only just remembered there's meant to be one. Which learning intention do you think students will pay most attention to and see most value in? I'll treat that as rhetorical.

---

47   Willingham, D.T. (2009) *Why Don't Students Like School?*

48   Sherrington, T. (2017) *The Learning Rainforest*

The wording

To help communicate the learning intention as clearly as possible, it needs to be carefully worded. Jargon and overly long phrasing should be avoided. Rather, we need learning intentions with **Stripped-back Language (TT4)**. They should be decluttered and jargon-free.

For example, consider the following learning intention:

- We are learning to use our active listening and teamwork skills to plan and carry out experiments involving pitfall traps to catch insects.

It is not uncommon to see learning intentions worded like this.

Compare it with this one:

- We are learning how to use pitfall traps to catch insects, specifically to:
  - Plan an experiment (in this lesson).
  - Carry out the experiment (in our next lesson).

This second version is more *specific*, is more focused on *learning* and has *removed unnecessary wording*. Use of 'active listening' (whatever that is) and 'teamwork skills' are irrelevant to *what* students are learning (these are about *how* students are learning).

Planning and carrying out the experiment are unlikely to happen in the same lesson. Because learning intentions should make clear the learning in a *particular lesson*, this needs to be made clear. Each learning intention will have its own success criteria (which we will discuss in our next section).

Power-up Prompt 2: The learning intention is *clearly worded.*

Give them enough time

One of the biggest issues I see in lessons with learning intentions is not that they aren't well worded, but that students aren't given enough time to process these when they are shared. The teacher displays the learning intention or tells the class what it is, but they do this so quickly that if a student were to blink or sneeze, they would miss it. This devalues learning intentions and strips away their potential to be useful.

Make them visible

In general, it is a good principle that students can *see* learning intentions, rather than just *hear* them. This means sharing them visually, via the board or a PowerPoint slide. Even if steps have been taken to 'declutter' their wording, they will still tend to contain a lot of information, much of which is unfamiliar. Displaying them visually should help to ease cognitive load, so students don't have to hold so much in their working memory at one time.[49] Rather than having to remember words as they are told them, students can see them.

In doing this, teachers should avoid the temptation to read learning intentions out *as* students are trying to read them.[50] Instead, give students a few seconds to read to themselves first, *then* read the learning intention to them, emphasising key words as appropriate.

Breathing space

If we accept that learning intentions are important, time needs to be dedicated to sharing them. **This does not mean that this should be spent with students copying learning intentions down.** Rather, it means students should be given some **Breathing Space (TT5)** to read these and think about them for a moment. If teachers have taken the time to *write them* carefully, it should be a given that students need time to *read them* carefully. Otherwise, what was the point in writing them?

> **Power-up Prompt 3:** The learning intention is *clearly communicated*, visually and verbally.

Signalling

Use of **Signalling (TT6)**[51] to emphasise key words in learning intentions can help to create 'learning hooks'. These are words and phrases that we draw particular attention to, and to which we want learning to link.

For example, if the learning intention is…

---

49   Weinstein, Y. and Sumeracki, M. (2019) *Understanding How We Learn*

50   This relates to **the Redundancy Effect**, which we shall discuss later.

51   This is based on **the Signalling Principle**, from: Mayer, R.E. (2020) *Multimedia Learning*.

- We are learning to **separate mixtures**, specifically to *be able to*:
  - Separate an **insoluble** substance from water

…then learning hooks highlighted by signalling are 'separate mixtures' and 'insoluble'.

If students already know something about these hooks, by drawing attention to them we 'activate' relevant schemata. This makes it more likely that new information will link to the hook. Hence, it is more likely that new information will be remembered.

> **Power-up Prompt 4:** There is appropriate emphasis in learning intentions to *highlight 'learning hooks'*.

Lessons as learning units

Just as not everyone agrees that the use of learning intentions is important (it *is*), not everyone agrees that learning intentions should be specific to particular lessons. Instead, some people believe that learning intentions could span several weeks' worth of lessons.

My own view is that the more specific a learning intention is to a particular lesson, the more useful it is. Like Doug Lemov,[52] I believe that each lesson should have its own learning intention. Both the teacher and students need to be clear about what this is. In the absence of clarity about the specific purpose of lessons, activities lose focus. Everything needs to keep coming back to the learning intention. Therefore, every lesson should have one.

> **Power-up Prompt 5:** The learning intention is *specific to the lesson being taught*.

---

52   Lemov, D. (2015) *Teach Like A Champion 2.0*

Summary

Element 2: Learning Intentions	
Power-up Prompts	**Trusted Techniques**
1 The learning intention relates to *specific learning, not doing.*	WALT (TT1) 'Know…', 'Understand…' or 'Be Able To…' (TT2) Pique Interest (TT3)
2 The learning intention is *clearly worded.*	Stripped-back Language (TT4)
3 The learning intention is *clearly communicated,* visually and verbally.	Breathing Space (TT5)
4 There is appropriate emphasis in learning intentions to *highlight 'learning hooks'.*	Signalling (TT6)
5 The learning intention is *specific to the lesson being taught.*	

Element 3:
Success Criteria

Success criteria relate to the *evidence* you are looking for to determine if students have learned what you intended. A useful acronym is WILF: '<u>W</u>hat <u>I</u> am <u>L</u>ooking <u>F</u>or'.[53]

Success criteria can take different forms, including:

- 'I Can...' Statements (<u>TT1</u>)
- Key Features (<u>TT2</u>)
- Exemplars (<u>TT3</u>)

Examples
For example, for the learning intention...

- We are learning about the structure of an atom, specifically to *know about*:
  – the sub-atomic particles that make up atoms

...success criteria could take one of the following forms:

'I can...' statements
1. I can *draw* a labelled diagram of an atom, showing the arrangement of the three sub-atomic particles that make it up.
2. I can *state* the charge of each of the sub-atomic particles.
3. I can *state* the mass of each of the sub-atomic particles.

---

53   Clark, S. (2014) *Outstanding Formative Assessment*

Key features

In the diagram of an atom you draw, I want to see the following clearly labelled:

- the nucleus
- protons
- neutrons
- electrons.

Exemplars

A good example of a labelled diagram of an atom is *this*; a less good example is *this*. The reason *this* one is better than *this* one is because...

Depending on what you are teaching, one form of success criteria might be more useful than another. For example, sometimes it can be difficult to communicate what success looks like using 'I can...' statements, in which case key features or exemplars would probably be better.

Sometimes, there is benefit in using a combination of approaches. For example, if the success criterion is...

- **I can** describe the formation of crude oil

...because there are specific points that you want students to include in answers, there would also be benefit in making clear **key features**:

- Your description should include the following points:
  - What it is formed *from*
  - *How long ago* it formed
  - Under what *conditions* it formed.

Power-up Prompt 1: Success criteria *clearly communicate* what you are looking for.

Sharing success criteria

While it is often useful to share success criteria at the same time as learning intentions, sometimes it doesn't make sense to do this. The most important thing is that, as a lesson unfolds, students become clear about what the success criteria are.

It is important that success criteria are shared in the way that most benefits the learning. Sometimes, that will be at the start of a lesson; sometimes it won't. Sometimes, there will be value in revisiting them at the end of a lesson; sometimes, there won't.

> **Power-up Prompt 2:** Success criteria *are shared and revisited at appropriate points* in the lesson.

Struggling with success criteria

Sometimes when I work with teachers, they tell me that they find it difficult to work out what the success criteria for a lesson should be. Whenever this is the case, I tend to find it's because they're not clear about what, *specifically*, they are teaching.

For example, I was once working with a teacher who was struggling to determine the success criteria for a lesson about places of worship. I asked him what the purpose of the lesson was. He said it was for students 'to develop an awareness of where people of different faiths worship'. However, he was not clear about what he was looking for students to do to be able to demonstrate their learning. Which religions did they need to know about? Was it enough to name the types of building used, or were students expected to describe specific features? If so, what were these features? It was a light-bulb moment: **clarity in relation to what is being taught brings about clarity in what students are expected to do to demonstrate their learning.**

Start by taking time to ensure you are clear about the specific knowledge you want students to learn, then work back to create success criteria. The development of Knowledge Organisers can help with this.

Assessment

A key use for success criteria is to guide the continuous assessment of learning in lessons. To do this effectively, success criteria need to be *measurable*. This means that they need to be *specific*.

A success criterion that reads, 'I can identify factors that affect the rate of chemical reactions' is not measurable, because it isn't specific enough. If, instead, it reads, 'I can identify <u>three</u> factors that affect the rate of chemical reactions', this is more specific and, therefore, more measurable. Accordingly, it is more useful.

Prove It

From specific success criteria, teachers can develop a range of **Prove it** (**TT4**) activities that can be used to assess learning.

For example, a self-assessment activity developed from specific success criteria might look as follows:

Success criteria	Prove it	Green	Amber	Red
I can identify <u>three</u> factors that affect the rate of chemical reactions.				

The 'prove it' column is essential if students are to avoid the traps of familiarity and overconfidence.[54]

Having completed this column, students can use their Knowledge Organiser to check what they have written. *Only then* should they evaluate their learning as 'green', 'amber' or 'red', informing the focus of their self-study programme.

Power-up Prompt 3: Success criteria are specific enough so that *learning can be evaluated.*

Avoid a group effort

Because the learning of every student matters, *all students* should be expected to prove their learning against *all* success criteria. This can only happen if there is evidence from *each student*, relating to *each criterion*. A group effort in which one student demonstrates learning against one

---

54   We discussed these in Learning Lesson 6 in Part 1.

criterion, and a different student against another, isn't good enough. Group success is not the same as individual success.

If differentiating success criteria – do it carefully

In the interests of trying to keep students' learning as close together as we can, we should take care in choosing to give different students different success criteria.

For example, if we use 'Everyone…', 'Some…' and 'A few…' terminology with success criteria, we guarantee that we will create a learning gap. It will divide the class and result in some students learning more than others.

That said, there will be times when different students do need different criteria. This will vary, depending on the context. For example, if you are teaching a music class where significant gaps between students already exist – perhaps because some students receive private tuition or are particularly talented at playing a particular instrument – then clearly it wouldn't make sense for every student to have the same criteria for success in a lesson. Sometimes, pre-existing gaps will dictate that a degree of differentiation is needed. You can't ignore a gap like this. The important thing is to keep differences as small as possible and to avoid them where we can.

Power-up Prompt 4: *All students* prove their learning against *each* of the success criteria.

Summary

Element 3: Success Criteria	
Power-up Prompts	**Trusted Techniques**
1 Success criteria *clearly communicate* what you are looking for.	'I Can…' Statements (TT1) Key Features (TT2) Exemplars (TT3)
2 Success criteria *are shared and revisited at appropriate points* in the lesson.	
3 Success criteria are specific enough so that *learning can be evaluated*.	Prove it (TT4)
4 *All students* prove their learning against *each* of the success criteria.	

Element 4:
Prior Knowledge

The importance of prior knowledge

Do these sentences make sense to you?

- NHS Test and Trace is preparing for nationwide 'surge' testing under which more than 400,000 rapid lateral flow tests will be sent by post to homes and workplaces every day.[55]
- Now is the winter of our discontent/made glorious summer by this son of York.[56]
- The conversion of l-gulono-g-lactone into ascorbic acid is catalysed by the enzyme gulonolactone oxidase.

If the answer is 'yes', it is because you have sufficient **prior knowledge** to make sense of them. If the answer is 'no', you don't.

Prior knowledge – that is, the knowledge we have stored as parts of schemata in our long-term memory – is **what we think with**. It determines the extent to which we can make sense of any new information. In the context of the classroom, the most common reason that students don't understand what is being presented to them is that *they lack necessary prior knowledge*.

Emphasising this importance, David Ausubel has said:

---

55   *The Times*, Wednesday 17 February 2021
56   Shakespeare, W. *Richard III*

If I had to reduce all of educational psychology to just one principle, I would say this: the most important single factor influencing learning is what the learner already knows. Ascertain this and teach him (or her) accordingly.[57]

Assessing prior knowledge

With this in mind, one of the most important things for teachers to do when presenting new content to students is to **find out what they already know**. This can be done *before* new content is taught or *as* it is being taught. A blend of both tends to be the best approach.

By finding out what students already know before teaching new content, teachers can:

1. **Make links** to this, making it more understandable and memorable.
2. Find out about **gaps**, so these can be filled.
3. Find out about **misconceptions**, so these can be addressed.
4. Pitch new content at the **right level of difficulty**.

Because every student will have different schemata – some slightly different and some very different – we need to take steps to find out *as much as we can* about the schemata of *as many students as we can*, within a reasonable timescale.

The simplest way to find out about what students know already is to ask them questions designed to assess this. We shall explore questioning in more detail in a later section of this book.

Beyond questioning, we can ask students to engage with tasks specifically designed to find out their prior knowledge. '**Spotlight assessment activities**'[58] lend themselves beautifully to this.

Spotlight Assessment Activities

Any activity that shines a light on students' prior knowledge can be thought of as a 'spotlight assessment activity'. Such activities are useful

---

57   Ausubel, D. et al. (1978) *Educational Psychology: A Cognitive View* (2nd edition). Referenced in: https://www.youtube.com/watch?v=AiL4AdmiHD0

58   Robertson, B. (2021) *The Teaching Delusion 2*

to teachers, because they **generate evidence** that can be used to inform teaching. They are also useful to students because they require them to *think hard* **about specific content.**

What follows is a selection of spotlight assessment activities that can be particularly useful in lessons.

KWL Grid

If we are starting a new topic, a useful activity to get students to engage with is a **KWL Grid (TT1)**.[59] The 'K' stands for 'what I already <u>K</u>now', the 'W' stands for 'what I <u>W</u>ant to learn' and the 'L' stands for 'what I have <u>L</u>earned':

K	
W	
L	

Students complete the 'K' and the 'W' at the start of the topic. The 'L' can be completed as the topic is being taught or at the end of the topic.

The 'K' helps to give the teacher feedback about what students already know, including any misconceptions they have. The 'W' gives the teacher an insight into anything students would like to learn about but that the teacher might not have taught otherwise. It can take the curriculum beyond the core. The 'L' can be used to generate evidence of the extent to which students have learned what the teacher intended them to learn.

Concept Cartoons

Concept Cartoons (TT2)[60] are designed to shine a spotlight on common misconceptions. With these, students consider what different characters in a cartoon are saying, including whether or not they agree with them, and why.

An example of such a cartoon in science is:

---

59   Naylor, S. et al. (2004) *Active Assessment in Science*
60   ibid.

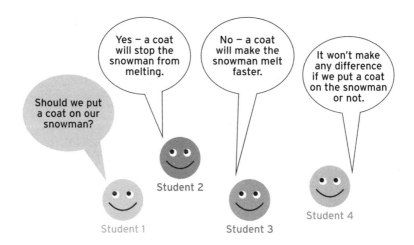

Examples in other subjects could be:

Subject	Character 1	Character 2	Character 3	Character 4
English	An apostrophe is only used when you have to shorten a word.	An apostrophe can be used before or after 's' to show something belongs to someone.	An apostrophe is only used after an 's'.	You should always put an apostrophe before an 's'.
Maths	When we divide numbers, they always get smaller.	When we divide by some numbers, they get bigger.	Nothing changes if we divide by 1.	If we divide by zero, we will always get zero.

True or False

True or False (TT3) statements can be *'closed'* (they have a definite answer) or *'open'* (the answer is an opinion and, therefore, up for debate). Both can be of value.

For example:

Subject	True or false?
History	Hitler became the leader of the National Socialist Party in 1921.
Science	When salt dissolves in water, it disappears.
English	The factor which has the most significant influence over Macbeth's actions is his wife.

The history and science examples are 'closed' true or false statements. They are designed to find out if students know the specific facts and concepts that they need to know.

The English example is an 'open' true or false statement. There is no definitive answer. Instead, it will bring to the surface a whole range of things that students know and understand, some of which the teacher might then choose to explore further. Open statements of this kind can also help get students to organise their thoughts, especially if they are expected to justify their 'true' or 'false' answer.

Odd One Out

Odd One Out (TT4) requires students to compare and contrast. The act of doing so gets them to *think hard* about specific content.

For example:

Subject	Which is the odd one out, and why?
English	roofs, roovs, roofes, rooves
Maths	0.2, −2, 2, 20
Science	HCl, H_2O, H_2SO_4, HF

As with 'open' true or false statements, there often isn't a definitive answer. But that doesn't matter – it's what you *find out* from students as a result of them thinking about these and justifying their decision that's important.

Empty Your Brain

When you ask students to **Empty Your Brain (TT5)**, you are asking them to write down everything they know about something. For example, 'empty your brain' about…

- Hamlet
- U-shaped valleys
- electricity
- rules for passing in basketball
- the last UK general election.

The openness of the technique can bring misconceptions to the surface, which might not have appeared using approaches that are closed.

Deliberate Mistakes

When designing **Deliberate Mistakes (TT6)** activities for students, teachers can use their pedagogical subject knowledge to get them to think about statements that include common misconceptions.

For example:

Subject	Spot the deliberate mistakes
English	Jim wasnt happy with Jill's response to the questions he was asking her.
Geography	To find out how far east or west a place is, lines of latitude are used. These lines run parallel to the Equator.
Science	The chemical formula for carbon dioxide is $CO2$.

Teachers can control the difficulty of such activities with the number of deliberate mistakes they include in each statement, and whether or not they choose to tell students how many mistakes there are. Not telling them this will get students to think harder than they would have to otherwise.

Multiple Choice

Like other spotlight assessment activities, questions that are **Multiple Choice (TT7)** can be used to target common misconceptions and mistakes.

For example:

Subject	Multiple Choice Question
Science[61]	The diagram shows stages in the production of a protein in a cell. DNA mRNA protein Which row in the table identifies the exact location of each stage? <table><tr><th></th><th>Stage 1</th><th>Stage 2</th></tr><tr><td>A</td><td>nucleus</td><td>cytoplasm</td></tr><tr><td>B</td><td>nucleus</td><td>ribosome</td></tr><tr><td>C</td><td>cytoplasm</td><td>ribosome</td></tr><tr><td>D</td><td>cytoplasm</td><td>nucleus</td></tr></table>
History[62]	History Liberal ideology: A. was invented in the eighteenth century to serve the interests of the British Liberal Party. B. developed as a hostile response to the emergence of industrial capitalism. C. is a compromise between socialism and conservatism. D. is a long-established creed which focuses on individual freedom.

They can be used to find out about prior knowledge relating to surface knowledge (as in the first example) or deeper understanding (as in the second example).

Because answers can be abbreviated by letters (A, B, C, D, etc.), they lend themselves beautifully to **Show-me Boards (TT8)**. Students can write their answer quickly, and teachers can check everyone's board in a short period of time.

61   https://www.sqa.org.uk/pastpapers/papers/papers/2019/N5_Biology_all_2019.pdf
62   Christodoulou, D. (2016) *Making Good Progress?*

Activating schemata

In addition to the benefits we have already discussed, there is one further benefit to learning that comes from assessing what students know or can do already. This relates to **schema activation.**

When assessment is used to get students to think about content they have learned already, particular schemata are 'activated'. What this means is that, in effect, these schemata are brought to the surface of long-term memory, so they can be pulled in working memory, as and when required. Although students won't be holding this content in working memory throughout the lesson, relevant schemata in long-term memory are *primed and ready* to accommodate new information.[63]

For example, if we plan to teach students about parallel circuits in science, there would be benefit in using assessment to activate their 'circuits schema' before teaching this new content. If we plan to teach them about greenware[64] in art and design, there would be benefit in first activating their 'clay schema'.

Thought about in this way, assessment is as important for getting students *ready to learn* as it is for finding out about what they have *already learned.*

Power-up Prompt 1: Assessment is used to *explore students' prior knowledge*, activating relevant schemata, and guiding future teaching.

---

63   Mccrea, P. (2017) *Memorable Teaching*

64   Greenware is the name for clay that has dried and is ready to be fired in a kiln.

Summary

Element 4: Prior knowledge	
Power-up Prompt	**Trusted Techniques**
1 Assessment is used to *explore students' prior knowledge*, activating relevant schemata and guiding future teaching.	KWL Grid (TT1) Concept Cartoons (TT2) True or False (TT3) Odd One Out (TT4) Empty Your Brain (TT5) Deliberate Mistakes (TT6) Multiple Choice (TT7) Show-me Boards (TT8)

Element 5: Presenting Content

Presenting content lies at the heart of teaching. It is through this presentation that students acquire new knowledge and skills.

The means by which teachers can present content to students are effectively limitless. They can talk to the class, with or without visuals; they can demonstrate something around a table; they can model something on a whiteboard; they can get students to read from a screen or book; they can get students to watch a video or listen to an audio recording; they can get students to watch their peers do something; they can get students to research something themselves. The list goes on.

However, just because content *can* be presented in a particular way, doesn't mean it *should* be. Some ways tend to be significantly better than others.

Presentation of content continuum

In thinking about this, it is helpful to picture a 'presentation of content continuum':

---→

Passive listening   Research

Copying   Discovery

At one end of this continuum, there are activities that require students to do nothing but listen or copy. Whilst listening *is* important for learning, listening for extended periods of time isn't usually a particularly good way to learn. When students do this, there can be an *illusion of learning*. They can *appear* to be listening; they *appear* to be engaged. But are they? Unless we are *interacting* with them continuously, we can never be sure. Copying anything more than the odd key word or sentence should have no place in the 21st century classroom.

At the other end of the continuum are activities that are unstructured and require no teacher input. These are the sorts of activities where students will often lose focus and go down blind alleys. They are the sorts of activities that tend to keep students busy and that many will enjoy, but from which little learning emerges.

The sweet spot is somewhere between these two extremes. **Interactive teacher presentations** that *hold student attention* and *make them think about specific content* are generally what we are after. Notes that students make during these should be kept to a minimum, so student attention isn't split unnecessarily. Students should never be copying extended chunks of information. If they need a good set of notes, their teacher can give them these.

Holding attention

No matter how interesting a topic being presented is, it can be difficult to hold anyone's attention for too long. The human mind tends to wander. As teachers, we need to be mindful of this. It's not a case of whether students' attention *might* wander – it *will* wander! It can be hard not to take this personally – but don't. It's biological. We just need to make sure that our teaching takes account of this fact.

Useful strategies to hold student attention, or to get it back after it has wandered, include:

- asking lots of questions to different students, but in such a way that no one knows who will be asked – **Cold Call (TT1)**[65]
- 'chunking' presentations, so that teacher exposition is broken up with short tasks requiring students to 'do something' with the information presented – **Chunk it (TT2)**
- varying the pace and volume of our voice – **Varied Voice (TT3)**

---

65   Lemov, D. (2015) *Teach Like A Champion 2.0*

- using silence for effect and emphasis – **Pause for Effect (TT4)**.

Each of these strategies involves some sort of 'change'. Change tends to help hold attention.[66]

Power-up Prompt 1: *Presentations are infused with interaction,* holding students' attention and making everyone think.

The quality of our resources

Influencing the extent to which we hold students' attention and make them think is the *quality of the resources* we use. Poorly designed PowerPoint presentations, tattered textbooks and low-quality video clips won't do much to hold attention, pique interest or communicate messages clearly. If students are to have the best chance of learning, we need to ensure that the quality of resources we are using to teach them is high.

Clean up your mess

In February 2020, I attended a researchED[67] conference in Glasgow. As part of this, there was a presentation by Robert Macmillan, titled 'Clean Up Your Mess'. It was about how poor presentation holds learning back. The messages really resonated with me.

Let's take PowerPoint as an example. PowerPoint *can* be an incredibly powerful teaching resource. However, like anything, we need to consider *how well* we are using it. **Just because information appears on a slide doesn't mean students will learn anything from it.** Learning just doesn't work like that.

Too often, teachers cram slides with text, much of which is too small for students to read. The colour clashes with the background. It all appears at once. We don't give students enough time to read it. We talk it through, but what we say isn't the same as what the text says. We include photographs, but these are too small to see. Some of them are badly pixilated. We insert ClipArt, but this just looks amateurish. As a result, teaching points are

---

66 Willingham, D.T. (2009) *Why Don't Students Like School?*

67 You can find out about researchED here: https://researched.org.uk/.

poorly communicated and students switch off, thinking about something more interesting. We need to do better than this.

Focusing attention to the right things

There is a balance to be struck between making slides visually appealing and diverting student attention from what's most important. Attractive slides are important, but more important is that students are thinking about very *specific things*, one at a time. Often, the most attractive slides are simplified ones.

Signalling

One way to focus students' attention is through **Signalling (TT5)**.[68] By making key words stand out, for example by putting them in bold, underlining them or making them a different colour or size, the teacher draws student attention to them.

Reveal slowly

Another way is to ensure we present information to students in small steps.[69] Rather than having all of the text appear on a slide at once, we can **Reveal Slowly (TT6)**. For example, we could:

- Use the 'animations' feature of PowerPoint, so that different points appear at different times.
- Rather than putting six different points on the same slide, use a different slide for each point.

Chunk it

The principle of small steps applies to any presentation we give to students, regardless of the form it takes. For example, if they are watching a video, it is important to break this up by pausing it at regular intervals and checking for understanding. This is the 'Chunk It' that we referred to earlier.

Text issues

For the next few pages, I advise readers to buckle up. We're going to be talking about some important presentation issues that are quite complex.

---

68   This draws on *the Signalling Principle*, previously referred to.

69   Rosenshine, B. (2012) 'Principles of Instruction'

You're more than capable of understanding everything, but be warned that you're going to be *thinking hard*. The issues we will be focusing on relate to presentations using text.

Bombarding slides

There can be a great temptation in teaching to bombard students with text. For example, when teaching students about vaccinations, a teacher presents the following slide:

> Pathogens are microbes that cause diseases. Immunity to a pathogen can be developed by using vaccines.
>
> Vaccines contain antigens from a specific infectious pathogen. The antigens used in vaccines can be inactivated pathogen toxins, dead pathogens, parts of pathogens, and weakened pathogens.

The teacher then does one of two things:

1. Read out the text, as written.
2. Talk about the content, but only make passing reference to the slide – what they are saying is related to, but different from, what is written.

Redundancy and split attention

Neither practice is good for student learning. The reason is that the information is being presented in the same 'modality' – in this case *words*, written and spoken – which students' working memory processes in the same way.[70] When both written and spoken words are presented *at the same time*, one of the two is redundant. This is often referred to as *the Redundancy Effect.*[71]

You might think redundant information isn't much of a problem: while unnecessary, it won't get in the way of learning. But you would be wrong. When we ask students to look at a slide of text, we are asking them to *read it*. They do this with an inner voice, which goes at a particular speed. If

---

70   Mayer, R.E. (2008) 'Applying the Science of Learning'

71   ibid.

the teacher then starts to read this outload as well, the chances of their spoken voice going at the same speed as the inner voice of different students are slim. It's not just that one of the two modes of delivery is redundant, it's that one of them actually *gets in the way* of the other.

The key learning point for teachers and school leaders is: **avoid reading out too much text from your slides.**

If the teacher is saying something different from what is written on a slide, this 'getting in the way' will likely be even worse. Now, students are having to split their attention between what the slide is saying *and* what the teacher is saying, which is different. This is an example of *the Split-Attention Effect.*[72] It will cause significant cognitive load.

The key learning point is: **don't expect students to pay attention to text on slides while you are saying something different.**

Breathing space

The Redundancy Effect and *the Split-Attention Effect* can both be addressed by ensuring students are given **Breathing Space (TT7)** during our presentations. For example, when new information appears on a slide, give students a moment to read this themselves, in silence, *before* reading it out yourself or saying anything about it. This will help reduce cognitive load.

Stripped-back slides

Returning to the slide about vaccinations, there are issues with the slide itself that are worth highlighting. These include:

- how much text there is for students to pay attention to
- how this text is set out.

Dense, crowded slides are not good for student learning. It would be far better to use **Stripped-back Slides (TT8)** that have less text, better set out. As well as being more attractive, these would be less likely to overload students' working memories.

For example, the slide on vaccinations could be presented as follows:

---

72   Mayer, R.E. (2008) 'Applying the Science of Learning'

Vaccinations

Pathogens – microbes causing disease

- Immunity

Vaccines

- Antigens
    - 4 types
        - Inactivated pathogen toxin
        - Dead pathogens
        - Parts of pathogens
        - Weakened pathogens

As well as reducing the amount of text, the layout has been used to help make key points stand out. Different points can be made to appear one at a time, using the animations feature of PowerPoint. This should also help to reduce unnecessary cognitive load.

Your voice is important!

Slides don't need to contain everything that we want to say to students, or that we want students to learn. We can use our voices too. Slides just need to summarise the key points. In doing so, they can provide *reminders to the teacher* and *learning hooks for students*.

By minimising unnecessary information from slides in this way, we are taking account of **the Coherence Principle**, which tells us that people tend to learn better when extraneous text and visuals are removed.[73]

The fear that some teachers have with stripped-back slides is that the slides will lead to stripped-back student notes that won't be good enough. However, this tends to link to a belief that students should be copying down the information from slides during lessons, which they shouldn't. **Copying information is a very poor way for students to learn.**

Yes, students need a good set of notes. But no, these shouldn't be produced by copying slides. We can give students prewritten sets of notes

---

73   Mayer, R.E. (2008) 'Applying the Science of Learning'

and make copies of our slides available to them. The time saved in lessons can be used for far better learning activities: those that involve *thinking*.

Transient Information

In considering all of this, please don't conclude that you should *never* read out *anything* that appears on a slide, or that students should *never* write anything down from a slide. That is not what I am saying. There will be times when both are necessary and of value.

For example, when teaching students anything new, there will be a lot of unfamiliar information presented to them. If this is all verbal, we need to keep in mind **the Transient Information Effect**, which tells us that having to hold words in working memory causes cognitive load. If key words and phrases are displayed visually, this will ease the load, because students have to hold less in working memory.[74] For this reason, there can often be value in students making a note of key words and phrases, which they can refer back to. This is the same reason why summarising key points on PowerPoint slides can be useful. We just need to ensure that we don't include more than we need to on these.

Summary

The key ideas relating to text issues on slides are summarised as follows:

---

74   Caviglioli, O. (2019) *Dual Coding with Teachers*

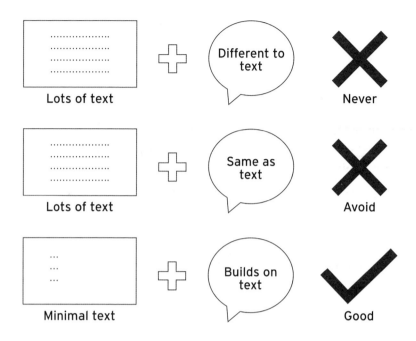

Verbal visuals

The issues of redundancy, split attention and coherence can all be addressed if we use **Verbal Visuals (<u>TT9</u>)**. This means combining *spoken narration* with complementary *visual images*, such as pictures and diagrams.

Visual images and spoken information exist in different 'modalities', which working memory can process *at the same time*.[75] What this means is that, when these are presented together, working memory can *process more* because cognitive load is reduced. This is often referred to as *the Modality Effect*.[76] It is summarised as follows:

---

75   Caviglioli, O. (2019) *Dual Coding with Teachers*

76   Barton, C. (2018) *How I Wish I'd Taught Maths*

The key learning point is: **presentations that *minimise written text* and *combine visuals with complementary narratives* should be a very good way for students to learn.**

Dual coding

As well as allowing students to *process more in working memory,* presenting information in complementary visual and spoken forms has an additional benefit to learning: it *produces a 'double memory trace' in long-term memory.* As a result, memory is strengthened and the chances of students being able to recall information successfully are increased. The effect is known as **Dual Coding.**[77]

Dual coding can come about in two ways:

1. Combining **visuals images** with *spoken voice* – this is the Verbal Visuals we were discussing

2. Combining **visuals images** with *written text.*

At the risk of getting overly technical, the second way can bring about the same benefits to learning as the first, because when students *read text,* they do so with a *silent inner voice.* Visual images and voice (this time silent) are again being combined.[78]

The key learning point is that use of **Integrated Text and Visuals (TT10)** – such as *labelled diagrams, timelines, cartoon strips, graphic organisers* and *infographics* – is likely to lead to better learning than use of text alone.[79] There is the additional benefit that this also tends to be more aesthetically pleasing.

77   Caviglioli, O. (2019) *Dual Coding with Teachers*

78   Based on private communication with Oliver Caviglioli

79   https://www.learningscientists.org/blog/2016/9/1-1

> **Power-up Prompt 3:** As far as possible, *visual representations* are blended with *complementary narration*, avoiding unnecessary written text.

Examples and non-examples

A key feature of high-quality presentations is the inclusion of concrete **examples and non-examples,**[80] with *appropriate explanations*:

- *This* is an example, *because...*
- So is *this, because...*
- *This* is not an example. The reason is because...

The more abstract the concept being presented, the more concrete examples and non-examples become important. They help students to link what their teacher is talking about to specific things *they can see*. As well as reducing cognitive load, examples and non-examples help develop schemata, establishing multiple connections that would not otherwise have been made.

> **Power-up Prompt 4:** Presentations include *multiple concrete examples and non-examples.*

Make it interesting

Students are more likely to pay attention and think about things we want them to think about when they find them *interesting*.[81] Making content interesting, particularly that which is naturally 'dry', is one of the key jobs of a teacher. (I will resist the temptation to suggest which content might be naturally 'dry' – no good will come of that!)

Authentic contexts

Sometimes, things become interesting when they are linked to 'authentic contexts',[82] by which we mean 'real life'. For example, when teaching the

---

80   Kirschner, P.A. and Hendrick, C. (2020) *How Learning Happens*

81   Willingham, D.T. (2009) *Why Don't Students Like School?*

82   Kirschner, P.A. and Hendrick, C. (2020) *How Learning Happens*

science of dilution, a teacher frames abstract concepts, like molecules, in 'real-life' scenarios, like diluting juice. However, not everything we teach *can* be made authentic, and not everything needs to be. As I discussed in *The Teaching Delusion*, abstract things can be just as interesting – if not more so – than 'real-life' things. Also, the danger with the authentic context is that students end up thinking about this more than the actual thing we want them to be thinking about.

Use of authentic contexts *can* make content interesting, but there are other, often better ways to do this.

Present a Problem (TT11)
People tend to like solving problems.[83] There is an in-built sense of satisfaction that comes from doing so. Therefore, to help make content interesting, there can be value in framing it as a problem. Often, this will mean asking a 'big question'. A 'big question' is one *that can only answered once a block of content has been taught*, perhaps in a lesson or perhaps in a series of lessons. Asking it at the start of a lesson can pique interest; answering it at the end can bring about a sense of satisfaction: 'We've solved it!'

For example, if you are teaching a lesson about the effect of particle size on the rate of reactions, you could start this by asking: 'Why is a flour mill less likely to explode if it includes extractor fans?'

In considering this, please don't equate 'Present a Problem' with 'problem-based learning'. 'Present a Problem' is a technique that can be used as part of broader teacher-led pedagogy. 'Problem-based learning' is student-led pedagogy, which is very different.

Tell a Story (TT12)
In *Sapiens*, Yuval Noah Harari suggests that one of the things that makes humans unique amongst living things is our ability to tell stories.[84] Told well, stories can be a great way to make content interesting. So long as they link closely to the content being taught and you make a point of emphasising and reinforcing key learning points, stories can also help

---

83   Willingham, D.T. (2009) *Why Don't Students Like School?*

84   Harari, Y.N. (2015) *Sapiens*

make content memorable. They contain hooks that can be helpful for developing schemata.

For example, if I want students to learn the order of planets in our Solar System, I *could* present a labelled diagram, ask students to take one minute to memorise the order, and then ask them to reproduce this from memory. This would probably be effective at achieving the learning goal, but it is a little dry.

To make it more interesting, I could also tell a story. For example, as I talk through the labelled diagram, I could tell students that:

> Venus is the second planet from the Sun and the third brightest object in Earth's sky after the Sun and Moon. It is sometimes referred to as the sister planet to Earth, because their size and mass are so similar. Venus is also the closest planet to Earth. The surface of Venus is hidden by an opaque layer of clouds that are formed from sulphuric acid. The planet is named after Venus, the Roman goddess of love and beauty, and is the second largest terrestrial planet.[85]

Much of the information in the story goes beyond what I want students to learn. In that sense, it is extraneous information. However, *all of it* has the potential to make the core content more interesting and bring it to life. Stories help us develop a sense of history in subjects, including the key people and events that have shaped them. As the teacher, you need to make a judgement about what the 'right amount' of extraneous information is.

The ability to tell stories tends to be linked to your knowledge of the subject you are teaching. If this is weak, take time in your planning to develop this. Your teaching will benefit. Planning doesn't just need to be about pedagogy.

Power-up Prompt 5: Steps are taken to make content *interesting*.

---

85   https://theplanets.org/venus/

Target memory

Sometimes, rather than rely on making content interesting, we have to target memory in a more direct way. This tends to be when students have to learn specific surface knowledge in order to develop deeper understanding.

Link it to what they already know

One of the most effective ways to do this is to deliberately make links with what students already know. The connections that are made to existing schemata should help students to understand and remember new information.

Analogies

This is why **Analogies (TT13)** can be useful. Analogies get students to link what they are learning to something they can already picture, helping them to make sense of it. So long as the limits of any analogy are made clear to students, the link to something they are already familiar with should support their learning.

Mnemonics

The same principle holds for **Mnemonics (TT14)**. These can help students to make sense of abstract content that on its own isn't particularly memorable, but that nonetheless needs to be learned to understand something bigger.[86]

For example, in chemistry, the prefixes meth-, eth-, prop-, but-, pent-, hex-, hept-, oct-, non- and dec- need to be learned to understand the chemistry of things like alcohol, vinegar and petrol. The prefixes are quite abstract and don't mean much in themselves. Unless they are being used a lot, they are quite forgettable. However, they can be made less forgettable if *associations* are made to words that students already know.

The mnemonic my chemistry teacher, Ms Richmond, taught us 25 years ago was:

- Monsters (meth-)
- Eat (eth-)
- People (prop-)

---

86   Willingham, D.T. (2009) *Why Don't Students Like School?*

- But (but-)
- People (pent-)
- Hate (hex-)
- Having (hept-)
- October (oct-)
- November (nov-)
- December (dec-).

In spite of the time that has passed, I still remember this vividly.

'Monsters eat people but people hate having October November December' doesn't make any sense as a sentence, but it *does* help us to remember the prefixes and their order. Often, the more ridiculous the better.

Build in retrieval

Another effective way to target memory is to **Build in Retrieval (TT15)**, both *as* new content is being presented to students and *after time has passed.*

For example, consider a geography lesson in which the class is being taught key terminology relating to climate change. This is the sort of potentially 'dry' content we mentioned earlier. Nonetheless, it needs to be learned. By building in retrieval, the teacher can simultaneously make the learning activity interesting and the content memorable.

They might do this by displaying the key terminology on a screen:

Key factors that affect climate:
1. Latitude
2. Altitude
3. Ocean currents
4. Topography
5. Solar radiation
6. Evaporation
7. Orbital variations
8. Volcanic activity

They then tell students that they have one minute to memorise as many of the terms as they can, and that they will be tested on the terms. Contrast this with a teacher who just tells students that these are the terms they will need to use and moves on.

Rehearse that in your head

An alternative means for students to learn these terms would have been for them to be told 'You have 1 minute to **Rehearse in Your Head (TT16)**'. Rather than students just looking at the terms for a minute, they are now deliberately going over these, using their inner voice to repeat them again and again. After this, the teacher would test their memory of them.

Instruct memorisation

Sometimes, there isn't enough time in lessons for teachers to target memory in this way. Instead, students need to spend time doing this at home. However, the teacher still has a key role to play by making this expectation explicit. Teachers need to **Instruct Memorisation (TT17)**.

For example, they might say: 'You need to spend 10 minutes memorising *this*'; '*This* is a key definition for everyone to know. I need you to make sure you have memorised it by the next lesson.'

If we don't, we are leaving it to chance, and it is less likely to happen.

> **Power-up Prompt 6:** Strategies are used to help students *memorise core content.*

Check for understanding

Students don't always understand what is being presented to them, no matter how clearly we believe we are doing this. Sometimes, this is because of their prior knowledge. Other times, it is because of how content is being presented. Often, it is because of both.

Once, I was teaching a lesson that involved students following a set of written instructions. I thought the instructions had been written very clearly. One of these told students to draw a table to record information and included the statement: 'Leave room for three more.' I was working with a small group of students when I looked up and noticed the classroom door open. A student had walked out. Confused, I followed him into the corridor and asked what he was doing. 'What I was told to do,' he said, with some indignation. 'By whom?' I said. 'By the worksheet,' said the student. 'It said I had to leave the room for three more.'

Believe it or not, this actually happened. The student genuinely believed there were three things for him to find outside the room to include in his table. The point is that we can never be entirely sure what students are thinking and learning.

Check, check, check

Accepting this, we need to check as often as we can that our instructions and explanations have been understood. The most effective way to do that tends to be by asking questions. We shall explore questioning in detail in a later section.

Also effective is to **Boomerang (TT18)**. Having given students an explanation or instruction, we ask them to give it back to us, either exactly as we have said it or in their own words. For example, you might say:

- 'Julie, explain to us what I've said we're going to be doing.'
- 'Christine, in your own words, tell us what the key points in that explanation were.'

This is a world away from saying to students, 'Do you understand?' and then taking 'yes', nodding heads or even silence as affirmation. We need to *check*.

Power-up Prompt 7: There are *frequent checks for understanding.*

Alternative explanations

Sometimes, we can think our explanations are crystal clear when the reality is they're not. What we say and what students hear are not always the same thing.

Frequent checks for understanding are the key to addressing this. However, checks aren't enough. These need to be followed up with reteaching, which will usually mean teaching in an alternative way. If some students didn't understand something the way you taught it the first time, the chances are they won't get it again if you keep doing the same thing. As I'm sure most of us have heard said, insanity is doing the same thing over and over again and expecting different results.[87]

Therefore, we need to come up with alternative explanations. The ability to do so is a key feature of great teaching and is dependent on the subject knowledge of the teacher.[88]

Sometimes, students are able to do this better than us. There is no shame in the teacher turning to a student who has evidenced they understand something and asking them to explain this to a student who doesn't. It's amazing how often students can come up with a better explanation than us! There's no need to feel insecure about this – take it as a compliment. Your teaching has helped someone else become sufficiently expert to become the teacher. That's a mark of great teaching.

> **Power-up Prompt 8:** Where necessary, content in presented in *an alternative way.*

---

87   This quote is often attributed to Albert Einstein, although he never actually said it.

88   Coe, R. et al. (2019) *Great Teaching Toolkit*

Summary

Element 5: Presenting content	
Power-up Prompts	**Trusted Techniques**
1	*Presentations are interactive*, holding students' attention and making everyone think.	Cold Call (TT1) Chunk it (TT2) Varied Voice (TT3) Pause for Effect (TT4)
2	Resources and presentations are carefully designed to support students to *focus on the specific content* that we want them to be thinking about.	Signalling (TT5) Reveal Slowly (TT6) Breathing Space (TT7) Stripped-back Slides (TT8)
3	As far as possible, *visual representations* are blended with *complementary narration*, avoiding unnecessary written text.	Verbal Visuals (TT9) Integrated Text and Visuals (TT10)
4	Presentations *include multiple concrete examples and non-examples.*	
5	Steps are taken to make content *interesting.*	Present a Problem (TT11) Tell a Story (TT12)
6	Strategies are used to help students *memorise core content.*	Analogies (TT13) Mnemonics (TT14) Build in Retrieval (TT15) Rehearse in Your Head (TT16) Instruct Memorisation (TT17)
7	There are *frequent checks for understanding.*	Boomerang (TT18)
8	Where necessary, content in presented in *an alternative way.*	

Element 6:
Practice

What we mean by 'practice'

Practice is about *putting into action* something that has been demonstrated or explained to you. For example:

- Having been shown how to dribble a basketball, students practise doing this themselves.
- Having had the concept of states of matter explained to them, students practise classifying different substances as solids, liquids or gases.

Sometimes, as in the first example, practice involves *replicating* what a teacher has modelled as closely as possible. Other times, as in the second example, it involves *applying* knowledge in different ways.

Regardless of the form it takes, practice is essential to learning. By engaging in practice, students develop schemata in long-term memory. By watching students practise, teachers get formative information about the extent to which they have understood what has been presented to them.

The link between practice and learning

While practice is essential to learning, it doesn't always result in it. Typically, there are three reasons why:

1. There *isn't enough* of it.
2. It focuses on the *wrong things*.
3. It focuses on the right things, but in the *wrong way*.

Whenever anyone fails to get better at something, it is usually the result of one or more of these factors. As teachers, it is important that we ensure students get enough opportunity to practise (in school and at home), know what they need to practise, and know the right way to practise it.

Deliberate practice

Often, the things that we need students to practise are the specific 'building blocks' required to do something 'bigger'. If writing a 500-word essay about the causes and effects of anaerobic respiration is the ultimate goal, practice activities should focus on developing the knowledge structure necessary to do this. They should not typically focus on practising to write 500-word essays.

Just as marathon runners don't train for marathons by running 26.2 miles every day, the same principle holds for students and what they are practising.[89] Practice needs to focus on *specific content* in a *targeted, deliberate way*. Later in the learning sequence, building blocks that have been developed through practice can be brought together.

> **Power-up Prompt 1:** Practice focuses on the improvement of *specific knowledge and skills.*

The stages of practice

In the earliest stages of practice, teachers need to be on hand to watch and guide. In effect, they act as a professional coach. As students get better and more confident at what they are doing, teacher support can ease. Ultimately, we want students to be able to practise and get better themselves, without teacher input or intervention. In other words, we want them to be independent.

With this in mind, it can be helpful to think of practice in three sequential stages: *guided, supported,* then *independent.*[90]

---

89   Christodoulou, D. (2016) *Making Good Progress?*

90   Rosenshine, B. (2012) 'Principles of Instruction'

Guided Practice

Guided practice is teacher led. It takes place *during* the presentation of content, as the teacher interacts with the class. The teacher *models* what they are looking for and provides *a series of concrete examples.*[91] The more examples there are, the more students will understand what is expected, and the more cognitive load will be eased.

Descriptive modelling

Guided practice tends to be best when it includes **Descriptive Modelling** (**TT1**). This means *showing students what to do* and *talking the process through.* By doing so, you make your thinking visible, articulating your inner voice.

For example: 'First, you do *this*. I usually concentrate on *this* to help me remember *that*. Next, you do *this*. *This* is easy to get wrong. A good way to remember how to do it is *this*'.

As this is being done, the teacher has the *full, undivided attention* of their students. Students don't have anything in their hands, they have their eyes on the board or teacher, and they aren't talking.

Scaffolding

Scaffolding (**TT2**) can also be an important feature of guided practice. By providing support and then *fading this out,* teachers can help students move towards independence.[92]

When teachers use scaffolding, they break complex procedures into understandable, manageable steps. This eases cognitive load. It's a bit like when we bake a cake and use a recipe: the recipe is the scaffolding. The more practice we have baking the cake, the less need we have for the recipe. Eventually, we don't need it at all.

Examples of scaffolding include use of:

- key word lists
- sentence starters

---

91   Hendrick, C. and Macpherson, R. (2017) *What Does This Look Like in the Classroom?*

92   Rosenshine, B. (2012) 'Principles of Instruction'

- exemplars (fully or partially completed)
- checklists.

Split Screen

A useful technique that combines Descriptive Modelling and Scaffolding is **Split Screen (TT3)**.[93] An example of how this might be used in maths is as follows:

Left side of screen (or board) – 'I do...'	**Right side of screen (or board) – 'You do...'**
Solve the following problem: 67×7	Solve the following problems: 57×7 97×7 107×7

On the left of the screen is a problem that the teacher works through, using Descriptive Modelling. A written record of the steps required to solve the problem is created. *This record remains visible to students* as they work through the problems on the right of the screen. This serves as Scaffolding. Once students have demonstrated they can solve a selection of problems with access to the scaffolding, it is taken away. They then attempt the problems without it.

Contrast this approach with one in which students are shown how to solve a problem, but the written record of how to do this disappears. The cognitive load for students is much higher, meaning they have less working memory capacity to think. As a result, they are more likely to get stuck and make mistakes.

Monitor and feedback

As we present to students, we need to check that they understand what we are presenting. A good way to do this is to get them to practise a similar example to what has been modelled to them. This will require a *cognitive leap*, with students transferring what they have learned from watching and listening to the example the teacher has just gone through.

---

93   Adapted from Barton, C. (2018) *How I Wish I'd Taught Maths*

The leap is unavoidable. The challenge for the teacher is to make sure that *everyone* can make it. Therefore, we need to *monitor closely*. Use of **Show-me Boards (TT4)** offers an excellent means to do that.

For example, I might model how to write a word equation for a metal reacting with oxygen. The example I use is lithium. Having done this, I will ask students to have a go themselves, but this time using magnesium. There is a cognitive leap, but a small enough one for most students to be able to cope with.

To check understanding, I could ask one or two to share their answers, or I could ask a student to come and write their answer on the board at the front of the room. However, both approaches would only give me *a sample*. Sometimes a sample is good enough, but usually it isn't. We need to know about *everyone's* learning. Hence, the use of Show-me boards.

I say to the class: 'On your Show-me board, write a word equation for magnesium reacting with oxygen.' I give them 30 seconds to do this, asking them to hold up their board when they are ready. Students know that it is okay to write '?' or 'I don't know', so long as they answer.

I move around the room, looking at Show-me boards, and giving **Live Feedback (TT5)**: 'That's good'; 'Perfect'; 'No – you've made a mistake there'; 'You've nearly got it – just be careful with *this*.' By doing so, I also get feedback, with evidence of understanding guiding my teaching.

> **Power-up Prompt 2:** Guided practice is used to *model success* and *gauge student understanding.*

A difficulty staircase

Based on what I see on Show-me boards, I will make a decision about what to do next. If there were lots of mistakes, I will return to modelling, pointing out the most common mistakes as I do this. If there weren't many, more likely I will ask students to practise another example, but one that is a little more difficult than the previous one. In this way, learning should progress via a **'difficulty staircase'**:

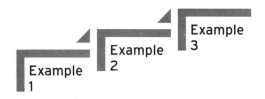

The success of students moving up this staircase will depend on how carefully the practice examples are sequenced.

As students move up this staircase, I will be honest with them that the examples are getting harder – it is important that they recognise this. As students experience success with increasingly demanding examples, their confidence will grow. There are few more powerful motivators than the experience and recognition of success.[94]

Should I realise I have moved to an example that is too challenging too quickly, we will take a step back and practise some more of the less challenging examples, before returning to the more difficult ones. You know that students are going to make mistakes at some point, so make sure you build in time for this in your planning.

> **Power-up Prompt 3:** Guided practice examples are *carefully sequenced by difficulty*, avoiding cognitive leaps that are too big.

The 80% Success Rule
Ultimately, I am guided by an **80% Success Rule**: I aim to ensure 80% of the class are achieving success in each of the examples they are practising, before moving on.

This is not to say that I think it is okay for 20% of the class to be left behind. Rather, the 80% Success Rule is a rule of thumb, intended to help me decide when to move up the difficulty staircase, or onto the next stage of practice, which is 'supported'.

> **Power-up Prompt 4:** Guided practice achieves an *80% success rate*.

---

94   Kirschner, P.A. and Hendrick, C. (2020) *How Learning Happens*

Supported practice

Having achieved 80% success in guided practice, teaching can move to **supported practice**. This is where students practise more independently and the teacher uses their time to **Circulate the Room (TT6)**, checking performance and offering support, where necessary. As they do, they are looking at student work and making clear that they are interested in it. They might make brief comments or pick a jotter up to have a look at it. In doing so, they can continue to give *Live Feedback* and encouragement. They do this as quietly and unobtrusively as possible, so as not to disturb the engagement of others.

Avoid unnecessary interruptions

Some teachers have a terrible habit of feeling that they need to interrupt students. This is particularly true when someone else is observing the lesson. Rather than allow students to work in silence, they feel compelled to *say something.* This harks back to a misguided idea that teaching must involve talking. It doesn't always need to. Sometimes, students just need space to practise themselves, with the teacher surveying what's going on.

Only if the teacher *needs* to say something – perhaps to an individual who has made a mistake or to one who is stuck – do they do this. When they do, this is in a **Hushed Voice (TT7)**, so as not to disturb everyone else. If everyone in the class needs to hear what you are telling a particular student, then stop the class and tell them this formally. If they don't, then you only need to speak loudly enough so that the person you are talking to hears you. Anything louder is often taken as a cue by other students to start to talk themselves.

Skipping supported practice

While supported practice *might* follow guided practice, it doesn't always need to. For example, following guided practice of writing word equations, I might decide to teach students how to write chemical equations rather than to move to supported practice straight away. To be clear: students *will* get the opportunity for supported practice, but I have decided that this would be more appropriate later in the learning sequence. It can be skipped for the moment.

The difficulty and complexity of the skill being practised should determine what happens next. If it is complex, or if students have found it difficult, there would probably be value in moving to supported practice straight away. If students have coped well in guided practice, or if they were practising a relatively straightforward skill, then supported practice might be better at a later stage.

Power-up Prompt 5: As required, *supported practice* is used to consolidate learning from guided practice.

Independent practice

Ultimately, students need to be able to do things on their own, without the support of their teacher or peers. Therefore, ensuring there is time for **independent practice** is essential. However, practice is only truly independent when the teacher isn't involved at all. Therefore, genuine independent practice is practice out of class, as self-directed study or homework.

Homework

Most students don't practice independently of their own accord. The intrinsic motivation just isn't there. Therefore, teachers need to set homework tasks that support this. Research tells us that homework, particularly at secondary school, has a high effect size.[95] However, for this to be the case, it needs to be the right type of homework.

Types of homework

Typically, there are three types of homework:

1. **Practice** – to consolidate learning from lessons
2. **Preparation** – such as reading or watching something in advance of a lesson
3. **Projects** – to enrich learning.

The type of homework we are talking about is the first, which should build on guided and supported practice opportunities in class. This

---

95 https://educationendowmentfoundation.org.uk/evidence-summaries/teaching-learning-toolkit

should include recently and less recently covered content. By doing it this way, we can utilise *the Testing Effect.*[96]

Power-up Prompt 6: Students are given the opportunity to practise *independently.*

Repeated practice

It should come as little surprise that *repeatedly practising* something is good for learning.[97] As we said earlier, one of the reasons people don't get better at things is because they don't practice enough.

Repetition can come about in two ways:

- all in one go – this is sometimes referred to as **'mass practice'**
- spread out over time – this is sometimes referred to as **'spaced practice'.**

Both mass and spaced practice can help learning, but not in the same way. Mass practice is generally better for *short-term learning*; spaced practice is generally better for *long-term learning.*[98]

This helps to explain why students who cram the night before a test can often do well, but given the same test two weeks later, they don't. The mass practice they engaged in helped their learning in the short term, but not in the long term. Short-term learning *faded* and, ultimately, was forgotten.

To avoid this happening, students need opportunities for **Repeated Revisits (TT8)** over extended periods of time. This draws on *the Spacing Effect*, which tells us that learning will be better when *multiple exposures* to the *same content* are *spaced out*, rather than back to back.[99] The act of starting to forget something, and the effort that is then required to retrieve it from long-term memory, has a positive impact on

---

96   We discussed this in Learning Lesson 8, Part 1.

97   Willingham, D.T. (2009) *Why Don't Students Like School?*

98   Wiliam, D. (2011) *Embedded Formative Assessment*

99   Bjork, E.L. and Bjork, R.A. (2014) 'Making Things Hard on Yourself, But in a Good Way'

learning. Therefore, it is important that teachers plan for spaced practice opportunities both in class and as part of homework.

Power-up Prompt 7: *Spaced practice* is built into the practice sequence.

'Blocking' and 'interleaving'

'Blocking' and 'interleaving'[100] are principles that can be applied to both mass and spaced practice. They are concerned with the *order* of practice activities within a practice sequence.

When we **'block'** practice, we spend a chunk of time practising one thing, then move on to a different thing, keeping this going. We don't return to blocks we have already practised in that practice session. When we **'interleave'** practice, we *break up* and *mix up* the blocks.

To appreciate this, imagine you are teaching a class how to name 'oxides'. Oxides are compounds that are formed when a substance reacts with oxygen. There are two different types: metal oxides and non-metal oxides. How they are named is different.

If you give students a set of five metal oxides to name in succession, followed by five non-metal oxides in succession, this is *blocked practice*. If these problems are broken and mixed up, this is *interleaved practice*:

Blocked practice	Interleaved practice
Name metal oxide 1	Name metal oxide 1
Name metal oxide 2	Name metal oxide 2
Name metal oxide 3	Name non-metal oxide 1
Name metal oxide 4	Name metal oxide 3
Name metal oxide 5	Name non-metal oxide 2
Name non-metal oxide 1	Name non-metal oxide 3
Name non-metal oxide 2	Name metal oxide 4
Name non-metal oxide 3	Name non-metal oxide 4
Name non-metal oxide 4	Name metal oxide 5
Name non-metal oxide 5	Name non-metal oxide 5

---

100   Kirschner, P.A. and Hendrick, C. (2020) *How Learning Happens*

While blocking and interleaving will both help learning, ***the Interleaving Effect*** tells us that **Interleaving (TT9)** can be more beneficial.[101] Having to jump between different thought processes makes students *think harder* than they would have otherwise, which is better for learning.[102]

The caveat we should put on this is that it is important that students have the opportunity to practise each process in isolation, *before* moving to interleaving, and experience some level of success with this.[103] If we move to interleaving *too early*, we risk confusing students. For this reason, it seems sensible that we avoid interleaving in guided practice, but build it into supported and independent practice opportunities.

> **Power-up Prompt 8:** *Interleaved practice* is built into a practice sequence at an appropriate point.

Different angles

At the start of this section, we said that practice is about putting learning into action. Often, there is value in getting students to do this from *different angles*.

For example, imagine you are teaching students to understand the life cycle of products. You have presented and explained the standard 'product life cycle' graph to them:

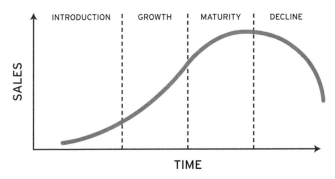

101   Kirschner, P.A. and Hendrick, C. (2020) *How Learning Happens*

102   Bjork, E.L. and Bjork, R.A. (2014) 'Making Things Hard on Yourself, But in a Good Way'

103   Lovell, O. (2020) *Sweller's Cognitive Load Theory in Action*

A short time later, you ask students to label a blank version of this graph. This is a form of practice. In this case, students are practising their ability to recall the correct terms.

You could leave it at that. However, to consolidate and deepen their learning, you could also ask them to:

- Draw the entire graph from memory.
- Spot the deliberate mistakes in an alternative version of the graph.
- Answer a set of multiple-choice questions, or true or false statements, about the graph.

By doing this, students are coming at learning from **Different Angles (TT10)**. They are having to think about the same thing, but in different ways. This helps develop and strengthen schemata. It also helps the teacher to check if students *really* understand what is being taught. The more things students are able to do with the content presented, the more evidence there is that they have understood this. This benefits both learning and teaching.

> **Power-up Prompt 9:** Practice opportunities require students to *think about content in multiple ways.*

Evaluation

In *A Quiet Education*, Jamie Thom emphasises the importance of *evaluation* in practice.[104] There is little point in students practising anything unless they are able to find out how they are doing with what they are practising.

Taped-up answers
In one of the first schools I worked in, I persuaded my Head of Department to buy class sets of multiple-choice quizzing books, supporting formative assessment. When these arrived, he insisted that the back of each book be taped closed, because he didn't want students to be able to look at the answers themselves. I thought this was a mistake. I *wanted* students to be able to check their answers. However, my Head of Department said they would just cheat.

---

104   Thom, J. (2020) *A Quiet Education*

Clearly, students *could* cheat. However, I argued that it is part of our job as teachers to create the conditions so they don't feel the need to cheat. That doesn't mean we need to tape up books! Rather, it means we need to teach our students to appreciate the importance of taking ownership of their learning and developing self-regulation strategies. This includes their understanding of the value of being wrong. However, because he was the Head of Department, he got his way.

I am sure he probably did find out that I cut the tape open the moment I was given my class set, but to his credit, he never brought that up with me!

Self-assessment

If we are to move away from students relying solely on teachers to evaluate their performance, we need to give them access to resources – other than the teacher – so they can do this. This is what **Self-assessment (TT11)** is all about. Making marking criteria available, including those from external examinations, is important if students are to be able to do this.

Being able to check their answers, students can take advantage of *the Self-Explanation Effect*.[105] This relates to research that has found that students who pause to reflect and explain things to themselves can learn more than students who don't.

For example, students might pause and ask themselves (silently):

- 'I wonder why *that's* the case?'
- 'If *this* is true, is *this* true as well?'
- 'What would happen if *this* occurs?'

It also lets students take advantage of *the Hypercorrection Effect*. This tells us that students who make mistakes with things they are *confident about getting right* learn more than students who make mistakes with things they weren't confident about.[106] As Mark McCourt puts it, the 'emotional shock' associated with this helps to 'dismantle'

---

105   Barton, C. (2018) *How I Wish I'd Taught Maths*

106   Butterfield, B. and Metcalfe, J. (2006) 'The Correction of Errors Committed with High Confidence'

misconceptions.[107] To take advantage of this effect, it can be useful to let students check their own answers.

> **Power-up Prompt 10:** Students have access to resources that allow them to *evaluate their own learning.*

Peer-assessment

Peer-assessment (TT12) can also be beneficial. However, on balance, I think the benefits are often less easy to achieve than with self-assessment. Self-assessment generates *internal feedback conversations* in a way that peer-assessment does not. Plus, students often lack the subject knowledge necessary to assess their peers and give them useful feedback.

However, this is not to say we should dismiss peer-assessment. It *can* benefit learning. For example, it can be a useful way to get over the limitations of there only being one teacher in the room. Students can't always see their own performance, and so need someone else to look at it. Also, sometimes students can be 'too close' to their own work, so are effectively blind to their mistakes. Peer-assessment can be useful in both scenarios.

So long as students have sufficient subject knowledge and understand the assessment criteria, they should be able to engage in peer-assessment and support each other's learning in this way.

> **Power-up Prompt 11:** Students have access to *timely support* as they are practising.

---

107   McCourt, M. (2019) *Teaching for Mastery*

Summary

Element 6: Practice	
Power-up Prompts	**Trusted Techniques**
1 Practice focuses on the improvement of *specific knowledge and skills.*	
2 Guided practice is used to *model success* and *gauge student understanding.*	Descriptive Modelling (TT1) Scaffolding (TT2) Split Screen (TT3) Show-me Boards (TT4) Live Feedback (TT5)
3 Guided practice examples are *carefully sequenced by difficulty,* avoiding cognitive leaps that are too big.	
4 Guided practice achieves an *80% success rate.*	
5 As required, *supported practice* is used to consolidate learning from guided practice.	Circulate the Room (TT6) Hushed Voice (TT7)
6 Students are given the opportunity to practise *independently.*	
7 *Spaced practice* is built into the practice sequence.	Repeated Revisits (TT8)
8 *Interleaved practice* is built into a practice sequence at an appropriate point.	Interleaving (TT9)
9 Practice opportunities require students to *think about content in multiple ways.*	Different Angles (TT10)
10 Students have access to resources that allow them to *evaluate their own learning.*	Self-assessment (TT11)
11 Students have access to *timely support* as they are practising.	Peer-assessment (TT12)

Element 7: Differentiation

Different and the same

Students are all different. They arrive at our lessons knowing and being able to do all kinds of different things. This is entirely natural and something we will never be able to change. Which is fine – difference is very often a good thing!

An exception is when it comes to students learning what we plan for them to learn. Here, difference isn't a good thing. We want *all* students to learn *everything* set out in our curriculum. However aspirational this aim might be, it is what all teachers should be aiming for.

This does not mean that we are aiming to produce clones. Far from it! Rather, it means that we want *all* students to know and be able to do specific things, *as a minimum*. In other words, we want *all* students to learn our **core curriculum**. This is about social justice and inclusion. It might take some longer than others, and some might need more support than others, but everyone should be aiming to learn this curriculum, in full.

Students will apply their learning from the core curriculum in different ways, both in and out of school. Some will extend it, others won't. Some will use it creatively, others won't. Such differences in how learning is applied are not particularly important. What is most important is that *all* students have the *opportunity* to choose what to do with their learning from our core curriculum. This means that all students need to have been taught it.

If we think it is okay for different students to learn more or less than others, this suggests we think it is okay for different students to have different opportunities once they leave school. I do not think this is okay. As teachers and school leaders, we should be doing as much as we can to ensure that *every* student has the same opportunity. This means that we need to do as much as we can to teach them all the same *core curriculum*.

Mutated differentiation

Hands up if someone has observed a lesson you taught and told you: 'You need to differentiate more.' Hands up if you have observed a lesson and suggested the same to the teacher. If your hand isn't up, I'm going to suggest that you are in the minority. Differentiation has become an all-consuming beast in schools. This isn't a good thing.

Like so many principles and initiatives in education, 'differentiation' has evolved into something it never should have been: it has undergone a **'lethal mutation'**.[108]

In theory, the principle that teachers should take steps to cater for natural differences between students is a sensible and equitable one. However, this does *not* mean that different students in a class should be taught:

- *different things* (that is, different curricula)
- *in different ways* (that is, using different pedagogy).

Sadly, this is often misunderstood. In a misguided attempt to 'personalise' the curriculum according to interest and preference, some schools advocate approaches designed to do exactly this. They are making a big mistake. Principally, there are two reasons why.

Consuming time and learning gaps

The first is that such approaches to differentiation **consume teacher time** to such an extent that it not only becomes unreasonable, but unmanageable. The perceived benefits could never balance with the very real costs. No teacher should be expected to differentiate like this. Ever.

---

108 'Lethal mutations' is a phrase coined by Ed Haertel, referenced in: https://www. dylanwiliamcenter.com/wp-content/uploads/sites/3/2020/10/DW02-01-Chapter-X-TLC-Paper-03-05-17-Digital.pdf.

Secondly, differentiating in this way **creates learning gaps**. If students learn different things, a gap between what one student knows compared to another automatically appears. If students are taught in different ways, some will learn in the best ways, and some won't. Common sense tells us this will also lead to gaps.

Ironically, gaps are the very thing that differentiation should be fighting to prevent. 'Equity of opportunity' through access to a *core curriculum*, and 'differentiation' as *different content and activities*, are diametrically opposed to one another.

The problems with a personalised approach

In a personalised approach to learning, all students *will* learn *to some extent*. However, this extent will differ from student to student, depending on what they are being taught and how. The gap between students who know and can do the most and students who know and can do the least will never be closed.

In *The Teaching Delusion*, I quoted Bart Simpson and I think the quotation is appropriate again here:

> **'Let me get this straight. We're behind the rest of our class and we're going to catch up to them by going slower than they are?'**[109]

In an equitable education, we don't permit gaps: we are aiming to create a level playing field. No matter what their background circumstances, or what they have or haven't previously learned, by the time they leave *our* class – *our* school – they will have had the same opportunity to learn the same core things.

The class as 'a unit'

To avoid the gaps we are discussing, we need to think about our class as 'a unit'. This means that, typically, we aren't going to have students learning different things or engaging in different activities. Some might be at different points within the same activity, but **as far as is possible, we are going to strive to keep the learning of everyone together**. Different students will need different levels of *support*, and some will be able to cope

---

109   Robertson, B. (2020) *The Teaching Delusion*

with more *challenge* more quickly than others, but we aren't going to start segregating students within our class and deliberately create learning gaps.

This is how we should be thinking about differentiation in schools: **differing levels of** *support* **and** *challenge* **as common content is taught.** We can reasonably expect teachers to be able to do this, and it won't create learning gaps.

The 80% Success Rule

Guiding our thinking about the class as 'a unit' should be **the 80% Success Rule** that we discussed in the previous chapter: before we move on, we want *at least 80% of the class* to be demonstrating success.

In the longer term, we will be aiming for 100%. However, achieving 100% in the short term is rarely possible. Natural differences in ability will mean different students master things at different speeds. A balance needs to be struck between taking everyone's learning forward together and holding back the learning of those who are ready to move on.

In the interests of maintaining an optimal pace, once an 80% threshold has been reached, teaching should probably move on. However, the teacher should clock which students need extra support at a future point. This might be during the 'supported practice' phase of learning that we discussed in the previous section, or particular students might be invited to attend out-of-class small-group tuition.

We aren't saying that we are okay with 20% of the class not 'getting it'. We are saying that, realistically, there will always be students in our class who struggle and who require extra support. We need to clock who these students are and ensure there are opportunities for them to get this at a future time. This is formative assessment in action.

> **Power-up Prompt 1:** The *80% Success Rule* is used to guide decisions about what to do next.

Access to support

At any point within any learning sequence, any student may require support. This can come from the **teacher**, from **peers** or from **resources** created for this very purpose. *Getting* the support matters more than the form it takes.

Getting stuck

Occasionally, I observe lessons where large numbers of students become 'stuck' at the same time and subsequently sit for long periods with their hand up, waiting for their teacher's help. A lot of learning time is wasted.

Such situations tend to arise when:

- Activities haven't been explained clearly enough.
- Guided practice has moved to supported practice too quickly.
- Students aren't encouraged to use their peers as a teaching resource – **Peer Teaching (TT1)**.
- There is a lack of support resources, such as help sheets, booklets and short video recordings, for students to access themselves – **On-hand Help (TT2)**.

Temporary Grouping

In cases where a teacher identifies a number of students sharing the same support need, it can make sense to use **Temporary Grouping (TT3)**. Here, students who are at risk of falling behind are brought together for a short period of time to be taught directly by the teacher. Those who don't require this intervention should engage in independent practice or an activity that extends their learning beyond the core.

Let's be clear: the teacher isn't planning individual activities for individual students. Rather, the majority of the class are engaging in a common activity that either consolidates their learning or enriches it. The minority who require additional teacher instruction get access to this before they fall too far behind. There is a temporary splitting of the class which, in actual fact, helps keep the class together. As soon as possible, Temporary Grouping is disbanded and the class reintegrates as a unit.

Out-of-class support

As we have already said, often there will be individuals or small groups of students who will need more support than can be reasonably given in a lesson. In this case, they should be given out-of-class support. This might involve extra work or attending support sessions with their teacher.

> **Power-up Prompt 2:** Every student has *access to appropriate support,* as and when they need it.

Challenge

As important as ensuring that all students have access to appropriate support when they need it is ensuring all students are appropriately challenged. When we get this right, we propel learning forward. When we get this wrong, we slow learning down. But what is an appropriate level of challenge?

Jumping ditches

To consider this, let's think about the challenge of jumping across a ditch. If the ditch you are to jump across is one metre wide, that's probably not much of a challenge. You could do it, but it wouldn't prove particularly satisfying or memorable.

Now consider a ditch that's three metres wide. Jumping over this is more of a challenge. It's doable, but it's not easy. It will require more work than a one-metre ditch. Rather than jump from a standing position, you will probably have to take a run at it. If you clear it, you will feel a sense of achievement. You will probably remember the experience more than you would have for a one-metre ditch. The memory is 'sticky', so if you come across another three-metre ditch in the future, you will feel more confident about jumping it. You might even be prepared to have a go at jumping an even wider ditch, your success having boosted your confidence.

However, if you had tried and failed to jump an even wider ditch *before* having success with the three-metre one, you might not have bothered with the three-metre ditch, deciding that you don't really like jumping ditches and you'll look for a bridge instead.

To move student learning forward as best we can, we need them to jump **Three-metre Ditches (<u>TT4</u>)**, not one-metre ones. Three-metre ditches are about *desirable difficulties.*[110] Jumping them propels learning *further*

---

110   Bjork, E.L. and Bjork R.A. (2014) 'Making Things Hard on Yourself, But in a Good Way'

128

and *faster* than jumping one-metre ditches does. Unlike what happens when the students jump wider ditches, here they won't fall in.

An example of Daily Review

With this principle in mind, consider 'Task A', which is an example of a Daily Review activity:

Task A

Match the name of each substance to its formula:

Carbon monoxide	NO_2
Carbon dioxide	CO
Nitrogen dioxide	CO_2

Completing this activity requires retrieval of knowledge from long-term memory. As we have discussed previously, this is good for learning. Therefore, we might reasonably assume that this Daily Review activity is a good one to start a lesson with. But is it?

I'm going to suggest it could be better. The reason relates to how challenging it is. This is a one-metre ditch activity – we need to try to make it a three-metre one.

With this in mind, I would like you to contrast Task A with Tasks B to D:

Task B

Name the following substances from their formula:

1. NO_2
2. CO
3. CO_2

Task C

Write the chemical formula for each of the following substances:

1. Carbon monoxide
2. Carbon dioxide
3. Nitrogen dioxide

Task D

True or false?

1. Carbon monoxide and carbon dioxide contain the same types of atom.

2. Carbon monoxide and carbon dioxide have the same number of atoms in their formulae.

3. There are more atoms in a carbon dioxide molecule than in a nitrogen dioxide molecule.

All four tasks involve the same knowledge. However, moving from Task A to Task D, what students are expected to do with this knowledge becomes progressively more challenging. By coming at the same knowledge from different angles, there is a progression in *how hard students have to think*. Accordingly, I would suggest that Tasks B to D are better for learning than is Task A.

An example of Plenary Review

Similarly, consider the following Plenary Review activity that concludes an introductory lesson on climate change, taught to a class of 13-year-old students:

True or false:

1. We are learning about 'the Bluehouse Effect'.

2. Burning fossil fuels is a bad thing.

3. Burning forests is causing climate change.

How wide do you think the ditch is this time? In my view, it's about one metre (or maybe less).

These questions do little more than skim the surface of student knowledge. They don't get them to think hard. We need to be more ambitious for our students than this. If we aren't, they will never fully realise their potential.

Guard against guessing

In an earlier section, we discussed the value of multiple-choice questions. However, an argument sometimes made against their use is that students can simply guess the correct answer. There is no challenge.

This is, of course, true – students *can* guess, and some will. However, there are things that we can do to reduce the likelihood of a correct guess. We can **Guard Against Guessing (TT5)**.

To appreciate this, consider each of the following examples:

Example 1

True or false: A bat is a mammal.

There is a 1 in 2 chance of a student guessing this correctly (50%).

Example 2

Choose the mammal:

- Crocodile
- Shark
- Bat

There is a 1 in 3 chance of a student guessing this correctly (33%).

Example 3

Choose the mammal:

- Crocodile
- Shark
- Bat
- Parrot
- Crow
- Turtle

There is a 1 in 6 chance of a student guessing this correctly (17%).

Example 4

Choose the 2 mammals:

- Crocodile
- Shark
- Bat
- Parrot
- Rabbit
- Turtle

There is a 1 in 15 chance of a student guessing this correctly (7%).

<u>Example 5</u>

Choose the mammals(s):

- Crocodile
- Shark
- Bat
- Parrot
- Rabbit
- Turtle

There is a 1 in 56 chance of a student guessing this correctly (2%).

The probability of a student guessing the correct answer (or answers) depends on how many there are. By not making this explicit, we make it even more difficult for students to get the correct answers by guessing.

Be honest about not knowing

Rather than have students guess a correct answer, we should encourage them to tell us if they don't know what the correct answer is. Saying 'I don't know' or drawing a '?' on a Show-me board should always be acceptable and preferable to guessing. A correct guess will disguise an underlying issue.

That said, there is always the risk that creating an 'I don't know' culture fosters laziness and a quick escape from thinking hard. The skill of the teacher is to tune into this and consider the likelihood that when a student tells them they don't know, what they mean instead is either:

- 'I can't be bothered to think about that.'
- 'I think I know, but I'm not very confident, so I'll say "I don't know" to avoid the fear of getting it wrong.'

This skill is rooted in knowing your students well.

Confidence measures

Use of **Confidence Measures (TT6)** can help with this. If students are asked to use a 2-1-0 system to indicate how confident they are in their answer – '2' meaning 'confident', '1' meaning 'I have some doubts', '0' meaning 'it's a guess' – it is more likely they will be prepared to give an answer instead of saying 'I don't know'. Being able to indicate they aren't confident acts as something of a shield.

> **Power-up Prompt 3:** Activities create *desirable difficulties*, getting all students to *think hard*.

Choice

As we have discussed, planning *different activities* for different students in a class is undesirable. An example would be preparing different worksheets for different students, depending on their ability. It we do this, we put unreasonable pressures on teachers' planning time, and we permit learning gaps.

In saying this, we need to be mindful that different students will likely grasp concepts at different rates. While we don't want some students to race ahead with others left behind, we don't want to hold anyone back either. A balance needs to be struck. *Choices* within activities can help to strike this balance.

For example, we might plan **common 'core' activities** for everyone, with opportunities for choice available *after* students have completed these. Those who need more time and support with the 'core' can get this while others have the opportunity to 'overlearn'.[111]

> **Power-up Prompt 4:** There is a *common core*, with *overlearning opportunities* that go beyond this.

Chilli Pepper Challenge

Sometimes, it is appropriate to let students make choices in relation to the support they access. This is a form of 'scaffolding', which we discussed in the previous section.

Use of a **Chilli Pepper Challenge (TT7)** is an example.[112] In this, support can be framed as 'mild', 'medium', 'hot' and 'spicy'. For example:

---

111   We discussed 'overlearning' in Learning Lesson 9, Part 1.

112   Clark, S. (2014) *Outstanding Formative Assessment*

Mild	You are allowed to look back at notes and work with a partner.
Medium	You are allowed to work with a partner, but neither of you are allowed to look back at notes.
Hot	You work independently, but you can refer to notes.
Spicy	You complete the task independently, without looking at notes.

Students should always be encouraged to work at the hottest level they are able to work at. If this isn't the 'spicy' level, at a future point in the learning sequence they need to be given the opportunity to do this: stopping at 'mild', 'medium' or 'hot' shouldn't be an option. Because of restrictions on class time, this might mean they have to do this at home or in out-of-class support sessions.

It is important to note that the learning intention is the same for all students. The differentiation comes from the level of support students choose to make use of at a particular time.

Pick and Mix

Another example of differentiation through choice is **Pick & Mix (TT8)**. With this, students make choices about the tasks they attempt within an activity. If a Chilli Pepper Challenge is, in effect, about choosing whether or not to wear arm bands or use a float, Pick & Mix is about choosing which end of the pool to jump into.

For example, imagine students in a class are to practise adding fractions. They are given 20 problems to solve. These have been carefully sequenced so that they go from 'relatively easy' to 'relatively difficult'. Students are told this. They are also told that they can choose which of the problems they answer, but all students must have answered problems 7 to 10 by the end of the 30-minute activity. This is the *minimum performance standard* everyone needs to demonstrate they have achieved.

Some students start at problem 1 and work through every problem, building their confidence. Some start at the beginning but only answer the odd numbered problems. Others start with problem 7 and continue from there. Such an approach involves differentiated challenge *within an activity*, helping everyone to jump ditches of the most appropriate width. The teacher hasn't prepared separate activities for different students.

Although different students are practising different problems, the choices they have are within a tightly regulated domain. In terms of the core content of the curriculum, the class is kept as close together as a unit as possible. However, there are opportunities for those who are able to *extend their learning* by tackling increasingly complex problems. Because there is rarely a limit to how difficult we can make activities, there is no need for anyone to be held back.

Guide choice

An important caveat on 'choice' is that students don't always make good choices themselves. Sometimes, they choose to do things because they are already good at them and more likely to be successful. Other times, they choose things because they think they will enjoy them, but actually, the less enjoyable choice would have been better for their learning. Therefore, there is often a need for teachers to **Guide Choice (TT9)**:

- 'I think it might be better if you did *this…*'
- 'Okay, I understand why you think that would be a good thing to do, but I think you're quite good at that already. How about you do *this* instead…'

Proportionate choice

By the same token, teachers need to be careful *how much* choice they give students. More choice doesn't necessarily mean more learning. In fact, it can often mean the opposite. Differences in the students' learning often arise from the differences in the sorts of activities they choose, and what they do in these activities.[113]

For example, I once observed a maths lesson for 16-year-olds in which six different stations were set up, with each station focusing on a different area of content. At each station, there were 20 different problems, each with a colour code according to their difficulty. Students were given the choice over which station they worked from and which problems they chose. It didn't prove particularly successful. Why not?

Simply, it was because there was *too much* choice, and the teacher didn't have enough control over this. Some students chose things that were

---

113   Nuthall, G. (2007) *The Hidden Lives of Learners*

too easy for them, and some that were too hard. Some chose things that they were already good at while some didn't, but it was near impossible for the teacher to know anything about this. They spent the lesson going from student to student, checking they were okay, giving pointers and answering any questions they had, barely stopping to catch their breath. There was no opportunity to get any sense of how the class was performing *as a unit* in relation to specific content. The differences between what they were all working on were just too big.

> **Power-up Prompt 5:** *Choices within activities* offer appropriate support and challenge to everyone, but keep the class as close together as possible.

'I'm finished!'

Sometimes, students get to the end of the activities we set them before most of the class has. What should we do with students in this scenario? We don't want them to be sitting doing nothing, and we don't want them to be bored by practising problems that aren't challenging enough.

Create Your Own

One of the things we can get students to do is write their own problems for another student to solve – **Create Your Own (TT10)**. By doing so, they will be applying their learning in a different way and tapping into *the Generation Effect*. This tells us that people often remember information that they *generate themselves* better than what they read about or are told.[114]

For example, students who spend one hour writing their own test questions can learn more than students who spend the same time answering questions from someone else's test.[115] Getting students to apply their learning by writing their own problems can be a valuable use of their time. The caveat would be that students need a minimum level of subject expertise in order to be able to do this.

---

114   https://en.wikipedia.org/wiki/Generation_effect
115   Wiliam, D. and Leahy, S. (2015) *Embedding Formative Assessment*

Become the Teacher

Alternative activities for students who have completed what their teacher has asked them to do include:

- Work with someone in the class who needs help – this is the peer teaching we discussed earlier.
- Create an information sheet that explains how to do the thing being practised.

In both cases, students are being encouraged to **Become the Teacher (TT11)**. This draws on the principle that in order to be able to teach something, we first need to understand it well ourselves. Often, we don't recognise that we don't really understand something until we start to try teaching it to someone else.

John Hattie reports that students who teach other students learn as much as the recipients.[116] Teaching someone else is therefore very useful for individuals to check and consolidate learning, and to maximise learning across the class.

> **Power-up Prompt 6:** Students who have *mastered content* are used as a teaching resource for others.

---

116   Hattie, J. (2012) *Visible Learning for Teachers*

Summary

Element 7: Differentiation	
Power-up Prompts	**Trusted Techniques**
1	*The 80% Rule* is used to guide decisions about what to do next.	
2	Every student has *access to support,* as and when they need it.	Peer Teaching (TT1) On-hand Help (TT2) Temporary Grouping (TT3)
3	Activities create *desirable difficulties,* getting all students to *think hard.*	Three-metre Ditches (TT4) Guard Against Guessing (TT5) Confidence Measures (TT6)
4	There is a *common core,* with *overlearning opportunities* that go beyond this.	
5	*Choices within activities* offer appropriate support and challenge to everyone, but keep the class as close together as possible.	Chilli Pepper Challenge (TT7) Pick & Mix (TT8) Guide Choice (TT9)
6	Students who have *mastered content* are used as a teaching resource for others.	Create Your Own (TT10) Become the Teacher (TT11)

Element 8: Questioning

When a layperson thinks about teaching, they tend to think of it as *explaining things* and *showing people how to do things*. To some extent, this *is* what teaching is about. If you can't explain something clearly or model it well, you are unlikely to be a particularly effective teacher. However, teaching is about an awful lot more than this.

Listening to what students are saying, and *watching* what they do, are just as important. It is through listening and watching that a teacher is able to determine what *they* should say and do next. Great teaching is *responsive*. This responsiveness relies on *interaction*. More often than not, this interaction comes about through questioning.

The purpose of questions

Asking questions serves a number of purposes, including:

1. Getting students to *think*.
2. Getting students to *retrieve knowledge* from long-term memory.
3. Checking students are *paying attention*.
4. Checking students *understand*.
5. Making students' *learning visible*, including *what they know (or don't know)* and *why they think* the way they do.
6. Getting students to *learn from each other* by listening and responding to each other's answers.

In 'Principles of Instruction', Barak Rosenshine suggests that **the most effective teachers spend around half of lesson time asking students questions.**[117] I suggest that, typically, for every minute a teacher is talking, we should ask at least one question.

> **Power-up Prompt 1:** Teacher exposition is infused with *frequent questioning.*

Not all questions are good questions

Asking frequent questions is important. However, not every question we ask is a 'good' question. Let's explore this.

The importance of background knowledge

Asking students questions can be a powerful way to develop the schemata they have in long-term memory, helping them to accommodate and assimilate knowledge in new ways. However, for this to happen, they need to have enough background knowledge to work with in the first place. If students don't have this, asking them questions that require it will be a waste of time.

I once observed a lesson where students were given a worksheet containing facts about the UK and Sweden. These included:

- average life expectancy
- longest river
- largest lake
- percentage of homes owned
- average gross income.

The worksheet asked students questions, such as:

1. Which country has a better lifestyle? Why?
2. Where would you prefer to live? Why?
3. Which country do you think is more likely to face problems in the future? Why?

---

117   Rosenshine, B. (2012) 'Principles of Instruction'

It quickly became apparent that students didn't have anything like the necessary background knowledge to answer such questions. The facts presented in the worksheet were insufficient to develop this. In their responses, students offered a sprinkling of *surface knowledge*, but to answer these questions in any sort of meaningful way, they required *deep understanding*, which none of them had. Students ended up writing a lot of 'stuff', little of which had much value. For example, to the second question, one student responded: 'I would prefer to live in Sweden because you live longer there, and it has bigger lakes.'

The activity was effective at keeping students busy, and many reported that they enjoyed it, but there was little learning from it.

> **Power-up Prompt 2:** Students have *sufficient background knowledge* to answer the questions we ask.

Getting all students to think

The example we have explored related to written questions. However, more often the questions we get students to think about in lessons are ones that we *ask them out loud*, as part of direct-interactive instruction. This is an essential feature of great teaching. The reason is because asking questions during presentations gets students to think about the content being presented in a way they are unlikely to have otherwise thought.

For example, contrast your telling a class that the temperature of Venus is 462 degrees Celsius with each of the following scenarios:

A. You ask students: 'How hot do you think Venus is?' A few students give different answers, and then you tell them the correct answer.

B. You ask students what the average temperature on Earth is. Everyone thinks about this and you ask two or three students for an answer. You tell students that it is 14 degrees Celsius. Many are surprised – it's not what they thought. The surprise makes this knowledge more memorable. You then ask: 'What do you think the average temperature on Venus is?' You give everyone 10 seconds to think. You ask a student to answer. Without telling them if this is right or wrong, you ask another student. Then you ask another student. You tell students that no one has got it right yet, but you'd like to know, through a show of hands, who they think is closest. Then you tell them the correct answer. Again, there is surprise. You finish by asking: 'How much hotter is Venus than Earth?' You give everyone 10 seconds to think about this before exploring answers.

So long as you ensure that there is clarity by the end, the use of questions to make students think will almost always help to make knowledge more memorable than it would be if students were simply told it.

Thinking challenges
One of the biggest problems teachers face when asking questions is students not actually thinking about them. The teacher is working hard, thinking of questions to ask and listening to what students say, and *some* students are working hard as well, thinking of answers and listening to peers, but many aren't. They appear to be, because they are sitting quietly, but actually, that's all they're doing. The reason is because they don't believe they are going to have to answer. This tends to be when:

1. A teacher accepts answers that are shouted out.
2. A teacher only asks students who have put up their hand.
3. A teacher uses 'call and response' approaches, in which the teacher asks a question, a student answers, the teacher tells them if it is correct or not, and things move on.

None of these approaches requires all students to think. For some, the work will be done for them by others. They get a free ride. But this isn't acceptable. **Every student should be expected to think about every question asked.**

> **Power-up Prompt 3:** *Every student* is expected to think about *every question* asked.

Useful techniques for getting all students to think about questions include use of:

- Show-me Boards
- Cold Call

- Pose, Pause, Pounce, Bounce
- 'Everyone Think About That'
- Catch
- On the Hook.

We shall explore each of these.

Show-me Boards

In *The Teaching Delusion*, I suggested that **Show-me Boards (TT1)** should be as integral to lessons as are jotters.[118] Actually, they should probably be *more* integral. Their use in lessons should be the rule, not the exception. They make every student think of an answer and commit to it, and allow their teacher to see this.

The only caveat I would put on the use of Show-me boards is that we need to take care with how much we ask students to write at one time. In a typical class of students, there is a limit to how much the teacher can take in from a set of boards being held up, even if this is staggered. A short sentence or a few words are usually fine. Extended answers or answers to several questions at once are less manageable for the teacher.

Cold Call

We referred to **Cold Call (TT2)**[119] in an earlier chapter of this book. With this technique, students are chosen at random to answer questions, meaning no one knows who is going to be called on. Accordingly, students are more likely to think about each question, because there is every chance they will be asked to answer.

For me, this is subtly different from 'no hands up' approaches. As I argued in *The Teaching Delusion*, there is often value in students putting up their hand.[120] For example, it can give you a measure as to how easy or difficult a class finds a question. You don't have to choose a student with their hand up to answer – that's up to you. In Cold Call, hands might go up or they might not, but no one knows who will be chosen to answer.

---

118   Robertson, B. (2020) *The Teaching Delusion*

119   Lemov, D. (2015) *Teach Like a Champion 2.0*

120   Robertson, B. (2020) *The Teaching Delusion*

Pose, Pause, Pounce, Bounce

Pose, Pause, Pounce, Bounce[121] is a four-part questioning approach:

1. **Pose** – you ask a question.
2. **Pause** – you allow thinking time.
3. **Pounce** – you ask someone to answer.
4. **Bounce** – you ask another student to comment on the answer given, and keep this going.

The 'pose' and the 'pounce' are effectively 'Cold Call'. The 'pause' and the 'bounce' go beyond this.

Pause

Pause (TT3) is about allowing thinking time. Rather than questions and answers being like a machine gun (*me–you–me–you–me–you*), the teacher pauses after each question asked and allows everyone to think.

Depending on the nature of the question being asked, the 'pause' could be anything from 3 seconds to 30 seconds. For example, if you ask, 'Which party was Tony Blair the leader of?', 3 seconds' thinking time should be sufficient and 30 seconds would be overkill. If you ask, 'Which of the policies implemented by Tony Blair's government do you think have had the biggest impact on society?', 30 seconds' thinking time would be more appropriate, because there is more to think about, while 3 seconds is unlikely to be enough time.

Often, there is no need to tell students you are giving them thinking time – you just give it by pausing. Other times, particularly when thinking time will go beyond a few seconds, there is value in making this clear. For example, you might say: 'Take 30 seconds to think about that'; or, '10 seconds' thinking time – everyone'. Doing so simply helps to reinforce that you expect that every student should be thinking.

Bounce

Bounce (TT4) is about encouraging all students to listen to and learn from each other's answers to questions. This is done by asking supplementary questions, such as:

---

121   https://www.teachertoolkit.co.uk/2011/11/04/pose-pause-bounce-pounce/

- 'Do you agree? Why?'
- 'Can you add to that?'
- 'Is she right?'
- 'Could you reword that answer to make it better?'
- 'There are some good words in the answer. It's not perfect, but it's getting there. Who thinks they can improve it?'

Catch

Related to 'Bounce' is **Catch** (**TT5**). Here, a student has given an answer and another student is asked to repeat back what was said, word for word. This has two purposes:

1. It checks students are paying attention.
2. The repetition helps reinforce what is being said.

For example, an exchange might go like this:

Teacher: 'What does the word "satellite" mean, Jamie?'

Jamie: 'An object which orbits a planet.'

Teacher: 'Thanks, Jamie. Marnie, repeat that back.'

Marnie: 'Um… an object which… I'm not sure.'

Teacher: 'Okay, well Jamie did just tell us. Make sure you're listening whenever someone is talking. Jamie, can you tell us what the word "satellite" means again, please?'

Jamie: 'An object which orbits a planet.'

Teacher: 'Thanks. Marnie: repeat that back.'

Marnie: 'An object which orbits a planet.'

Teacher: 'Good. Fiona, repeat that back.'

Fiona: 'An object which orbits a planet.'

Teacher: 'Good. Right, everyone: repeat that back together, on three. Three, two, one…'

Everyone: 'An object which orbits a planet.'

Teacher: 'Perfect. A satellite is an object which orbits a planet. We all need to know that.'

On the Hook

Sometimes students believe that, because they have just answered a question, they won't be chosen to answer another one, at least not any time soon. Instead, because they've just answered, the teacher will ask other students. This gives them a mandate to 'switch off' and stop paying attention as closely.

To stop this from happening, they need to be kept **On the Hook** (**TT6**). Instead of ticking off a student as 'done' after having answered a question, the teacher makes a mental note to go back to this student again a short time later.

Explore thinking

A common temptation in teaching is to jump from question to question as quickly as possible. Lots of questions are asked, and lots of students are asked to answer these, but only *surface knowledge* is assessed. Sometimes, good surface knowledge hides issues that exist deeper down.

For example, you ask a student, 'Is sodium hydroxide solution acidic or alkaline?' The student says, 'Alkaline.' They might have got this correct for the right reasons, but they might not – they might have just guessed, or they might have got it correct via a misconception. As teachers, we need to find this out.

Drill Down

If you follow the question up with, 'Why do you think that?' and they say, 'Because it's got sodium in it and everything with sodium in it is alkaline,' then you know that they got the answer correct but for the wrong reason. A better answer to this question would have been: 'Because it's a metal hydroxide, and metal hydroxide solutions are always alkaline.'

This is about taking time to **Drill Down** (**TT7**) into student thinking as part of questioning. Rather than accepting an answer and telling students if it is right or wrong straight away, it is more formative to drill beneath the surface and find out *why students said what they did or what else they know about this.* Doing so can help to unearth deep-rooted misconceptions that might not otherwise have been uncovered.

Drilling down takes more time, but it is always time well spent. It requires use of questions designed for this purpose. 'Why?' is a ubiquitous drill-down question. So too are the following:

- 'Can you say a bit more about that?'
- 'What makes you so sure about that?'
- 'Okay, so you're saying *this*, but would it be fair to say *this*?'

Comparisons

Use of comparisons is often an effective means to drill down. For example, consider the following two questions:

A. Is a bat a mammal?

B. Why is a bat a mammal but a penguin isn't?

The need to *compare* in Question B makes it a better 'drilling-down' question than Question A because it naturally lends itself to: 'Why?' Students are being forced to think about this.

Statements, rather than questions

Sometimes, it is better to ask students to think about statements rather than questions. For example, compare A with B:

A. Which country was responsible for the outbreak of World War I?

B. Russia was responsible for the outbreak of World War I – discuss.

'A' is good for assessing surface knowledge, but it tells you nothing about knowledge that sits underneath. 'B' is much better for doing that.

Power-up Prompt 4: Questioning is used to explore both *surface knowledge* and *deep understanding.*

Listen to what students say

Asking questions isn't just about *getting students to think* – it is also about *the teacher finding out what students are thinking.* This means listening to their answers, carefully.

Recently, I observed a science lesson about climate change. In an introductory activity, some photographs were projected onto the screen and students were asked to think about what each had to do with climate change. One of these was of a factory producing emissions. After 20 seconds' thinking time, a student was asked for their answer. 'It's producing fossil fuels,' he said. 'That's right – well done!' said the teacher, moving on to the next photograph.

The student had correctly identified that the picture had something to do with fossil fuels. However, incorrectly, he said the factory was *producing* fossil fuels. It wasn't: it was *burning* fossil fuels and *producing* carbon dioxide (which is linked to climate change). Working on the assumption that the teacher knew this himself, he simply didn't listen carefully enough to the student's answer. As a result, this student was left with the wrong idea, along with the rest of the class. Instead of responding to the student's misconception, the teacher reinforced it. I don't intend to be too blunt, but this isn't *teaching*. Dare I say, it's actually the opposite.

Homing In

It is not uncommon for me to watch a lesson in which the teacher asks a question, a student gives an answer with a loose link to a correct one, and the teacher says, 'Good', 'That's right' or 'Well done' before moving on. Yes, it's good that an answer was given. And no, we shouldn't berate students for wrong answers – we should welcome them and use them as opportunities to learn. But we *do* need to help students to improve and correct imperfect answers.

Often, this means **Homing in (TT8)** on particular words and phrases, to give feedback, to ask other students to comment, or to correct errors ourselves. For example, in the case of the lesson we were just exploring, better responses from the teacher could have been:

- 'It's got something to do with fossil fuels, Martin, but "producing" isn't quite right. Can you have another go?'
- 'That's getting close, Martin, but there's one word in that answer that's not quite right. Can you think what it is?'
- 'You are right to highlight "fossil fuels", Martin. That's good. But "producing" isn't the right word. Can you think of a better one?'

- 'Would anyone like to comment on what Martin has just said?'

> **Power-up Prompt 5:** Through *careful listening*, teaching engages with students' answers, including the *specific detail* of these.

Students listening to each other

Almost every exchange between teacher and student is an opportunity for *everyone* to learn. For this to happen, everyone needs to be listening to the teacher, and everyone needs to be listening to every student. Very few exchanges need to be private.

However, too often this isn't the case. Too often, when a student is answering a teacher's question, other students aren't listening. This tends to be because:

1. They don't believe they need to be listening.
2. They can't hear what the other student is saying.

Establish an expectation

To avoid the first of these, we need to establish conditions in which every student knows that they are expected to listen to the answer of every other student. Reinforcing a principle of politeness is a good start.

Turn up the volume

To avoid the second, it will often be necessary to do something to help make a student's answer audible to everyone else. One way to do this is to ask students to **Say it Again, Louder (TT9)**. In doing so, we should be mindful that some students will be shy and won't like speaking out in front of their peers. What we need to do is ensure we have created the conditions in which students don't feel fear in doing so. They know that their answer will be listened to and valued – it will never be used to mock or humiliate anyone.

Another way to do this is to **Amplify (TT10)** student answers. When we do this, we repeat the answer back, word for word, so that everyone can hear it. The temptation is often to paraphrase, to summarise or to correct errors in a student's answer. But that's not what should happen. Instead, the answer should be repeated so that everyone hears it, exactly as it was.

Hearing it back, the student might want to correct something that they recognise they've got wrong. If and when the opportunity arises for them to do that, they should be given it.

> **Power-up Prompt 6:** Students listen to and learn from *each other's answers.*

'I don't know'

Sometimes, students don't know the answer to the questions we ask them. This is okay, so long as they understand that they need to now do something to make sure that, when asked this question again, they should know.

For example, imagine you ask, 'What are the key differences between a developed and a developing country, Avril?' Avril replies, 'I'm not sure.'

Believing this response is due to a lack of confidence, you might push Avril a little, saying something like, 'Try to have a go.' Avril might then come out with a good answer or part of a good answer, which you can build on. However, she might also repeat, 'I'm not sure.' What should you do at this point?

I know some teachers who would say, 'Well you *should* know.' I am certain I have done this myself. However, this response is unlikely to do much to help Avril's learning. What is more likely to help is if you accept that Avril doesn't know but say, **'I'll Come Back to You' (TT11)**. You direct the question to another student. Once you get a correct answer, you go back to Avril and ask her to have a go again now.

Alternatively, you might offer Avril the opportunity to **Phone a Friend (TT12)**. By doing so, she would have the chance to ask a peer to offer an answer for her. Assuming they give a correct answer, it would then be important to use the Catch technique we discussed earlier to check that Avril has listened carefully. Otherwise, she might just have thrown her friend under a bus and run away.

Should you find out that Avril is not alone and very few students are able to answer the questions you are asking, you might say something like: 'I don't think everyone knows this as well as they should. Before our next lesson, I want you to spend ten minutes doing some revision on the difference between developed and developing countries. I am going to ask you about this again in the next lesson and I expect everyone to be able to answer the questions I ask.' You **Instruct Memorisation (TT13)**.

Power-up Prompt 7: Students who can't answer questions are *supported and challenged* to learn what they need to answer these in future.

Summary

Element 8: Questioning	
Power-up Prompts	**Trusted Techniques**
1	Teacher exposition is infused with *frequent questioning*.	
2	Students have *sufficient background knowledge* to answer the questions we ask.	
3	*Every student* is expected to think about *every question* asked.	Show-me Boards (TT1) Cold Call (TT2) Pause (TT3) Bounce (TT4) Catch (TT5) On the Hook (TT6)
4	Questioning is used to explore both *surface knowledge* and *deep understanding*.	Drill Down (TT7)
5	Through *careful listening*, teaching engages with students' answers, including the *specific detail* of these.	Homing in (TT8)
6	Students listen to and learn from *each other's answers*.	Say it Again, Louder (TT9) Amplify (TT10)

Element 8: Questioning	
Power-up Prompts	**Trusted Techniques**
7	Students who can't answer questions are *supported and challenged* to learn what they need to answer these in future.	I'll Come Back to You (TT11) Phone a Friend (TT12) Instruct Memorisation (TT13)

Element 9: Discussion

Students can learn a great deal by discussing things. When they discuss, they have to *verbalise* their thinking, which can help clarify it. They also have to *listen* to other people and consider to what extent they agree or disagree with what is being said. Again, this can clarify thinking.

Someone might say something that a student hadn't thought of themselves. Someone might say something in a way that really resonates with them. Sometimes, students learn more from each other during discussion than they do from their teacher or from reading about a topic.[122]

How much students learn through discussion depends on:

1. *How much they already know* about what they are discussing.

2. *How focused* the discussion is.

Asking students to discuss 'What do you think it is like to live in China?' will be a waste of time if students don't know anything about China, or if they are just left to talk about anything they want to. Discussion *can* advance learning. However, managed poorly, it can quickly become another 'being busy activity'.[123]

> **Power-up Prompt 1:** Students have sufficient *background knowledge* to participate in discussions.

---

122 Nuthall, G. (2007) *The Hidden Lives of Learners*
123 We referred to this in the chapter on Daily Review.

Assuming students do have adequate knowledge to learn through discussion, the more focused the discussion is, the more productive it is likely to be. To ensure this is the case, you should give students a specific steer, such as:

- I want you to discuss *this*, *this* and *this*.
- By the end of your discussion, I expect *this*.

Doing so should prevent discussions going off topic and drifting.

Power-up Prompt 2: Discussions are *focused on specific learning.*

Whole-class discussion vs small-group discussion

A common delusion in the teaching profession is that to discuss things, students need to work in groups. They don't. Whole-class discussion, led by the teacher, is often a far richer learning experience for students. Detractors of so-called 'teacher-led' learning often miss this point. It's not 'teacher-only' learning. While there *can* be value in small-group discussion, there is often more in discussion as a whole class.

Creating the conditions

Regardless of whether discussion is whole class or small group, for it to impact positively on the learning of all students, the conditions have to be carefully established and controlled. These include that:

- *One person* speaks at a time.
- *All students* listen to whoever is talking.
- *No student* should ever make fun of another for what they say.

Participation

Not every student feels comfortable contributing to discussion. They may have a valuable point to make, but, for whatever reason, they won't make it unless the teacher does something to **Invite Them in (TT1)**.

To manage this, teachers need to be mindful of who has said a lot and who hasn't said anything. Subtle prompts like, 'Francesca, do you have anything you'd like to say about that?', can be effective for getting shyer students to speak. So too can lines like, 'You've made several good contributions, Peter. Now I'd like to hear from someone else.'

Controlled turns

This last point also relates to the principle of **Controlled Turns (TT2)**. As they manage whole-class discussion, teachers need to take care not to let particular students dominate, or to let students interrupt or speak over each other.

Controlled Turns are just as important in small-group discussion. To manage this, the teacher could assign different letters to students – A, B, C, etc. – and give direction as to whose turn it is to speak at a particular time. 'Okay, that's enough time for the As. I'd now like everyone who is a B to take a turn at speaking.'

Focus on pairs

When teachers ask questions designed to explore deep understanding (as opposed to surface knowledge), or questions that they believe are particularly challenging, there can be value in asking students to **Chat to a Partner (TT3)**. Doing so creates thinking time and allows students to bounce points off one another before sharing these in front of the class. This can help to build confidence and encourage students to speak out.

For example, a teacher might ask: 'What is the difference between the House of Commons and the House of Lords?' They could ask students to note key points on a Show-me board. Or they could Cold Call students. However, they could also say 'Chat to a Partner'. As students do this, the teacher can circulate the room and listen in to conversations. By doing so, they are able to get formative information about what different students think.

After a set period of time, the teacher can invite students to share what they were discussing with the whole class. In this way, students learn in small groups *and* from the class as a whole.

Power-up Prompt 3: Discussions are managed so *all students* participate and learn from each other.

Repetition

As discussed in the previous chapter on questioning, sometimes the teacher will need to ask students to **Say it Again, Louder (TT4)**, or **Amplify (TT5)** points for them. This is about both ensuring everyone hears what has been said and adding weight to particular points: 'That's a really important point that Jennifer has just made. Jennifer – would you mind repeating it, please? I want everyone to hear that.'

Clarification

Sometimes, we will need to ask students to make **Polished-up Points (TT6)**. They have made a contribution to the discussion, but it's not entirely clear what they meant by this. Being honest with students and helping them to make their point clearer is important if we are to avoid misconceptions developing and taking root. This takes more time, but it is usually time well spent.

Chart it

Whole-class discussion asks a lot of working memory. As it unfolds, a wide range of key words and phrases will emerge. Points will get made that are important for all students to know. Points will also get made that are wrong. Many points will be useful to refer back to later in the discussion.

If we don't write any of this down, we are putting huge demands on the memory of both students and ourselves. Words are transient, meaning unless we hold them in working memory, or store them in long-term memory, they disappear. This is *the Transient Information Effect* that we discussed in an earlier section.

To help address this, we can use a board, flip chart or screen to **Chart it (TT7)**. As key points get made, they can be written down for everyone to see and refer back to. For example, in a discussion about the electromagnetic spectrum, we might chart the terms 'x-rays', 'wavelength', 'frequency', 'ultraviolet' and 'infrared' as they are mentioned.

As well as easing cognitive load, this helps to prevent misunderstandings that can result from unfamiliar words being heard but not seen, or the opposite. For example, the word 'infrared' might get said, but if the teacher doesn't Chart it, some students might mishear this as 'inferred', which would lead to misunderstanding. In charting words, the teacher should ensure all students have heard them aloud, so they know how to pronounce them.

> **Power-up Prompt 4:** *Key points* that emerge from discussions are *emphasised* and *made clear.*

Thinking for themselves

One of our goals as teachers is to support students to think for themselves. We do this by teaching them a broad, deep body of knowledge, which they can use to think with. Sometimes, this will mean teaching them about things that we don't believe in ourselves.

For example, we may not be in favour of capitalism or socialism, but students need to develop knowledge of such things so that they can understand what is being reported in newspapers, on TV and via social media. They need to be able to form their *own views* on such matters.

Accordingly, we should be careful not to betray our own biases. There is a difference between being honest with students by making clear which side of a debate we are on and trying to persuade students to form one view or another based on our own beliefs.

Correcting students

In the course of thinking for themselves, sometimes students will express an opinion that has the potential to cause offence. Any time this happens, teachers need to challenge it. While freedom of speech is an important principle, it can never be used as an excuse to tolerate offensive remarks. It is an important part of our job as teachers to educate students about the relationship between the two. We need to act as positive role models.

> **Power-up Prompt 5:** There is due care to *avoid teaching biases or allowing offence to be caused.*

Summary

Element 9: Discussion	
Power-up Prompts	**Trusted Techniques**
1 Students have sufficient *background knowledge* to participate in discussions.	
2 Discussions are *focused on specific learning.*	Invite Them in (TT1) Controlled Turns (TT2) Chat to a Partner (TT3)
3 Discussions are managed so *all students* participate and learn from each other.	Say it Again, Louder (TT4) Amplify (TT5) Polished-up Points (TT6) Chart it (TT7)
4 *Key points* that emerge from discussions are *emphasised* and *made clear.*	
5 There is due care to *avoid teaching biases or allowing offence to be caused.*	

Element 10: Feedback

While learning *can* happen without feedback, it will always tend to be better when feedback is involved. The less expert anyone is in any area, the more important is feedback from an expert.

Feedback is top of the list of the Education Endowment Foundation's practices that make the biggest difference to student learning.[124]

The practice–feedback loop

My golf doesn't tend to improve for two reasons. The first is that I *don't practise enough*. The second is that, when I do practise, I often practise things I think are right, but actually aren't. I *groove faults*. I would do far better if I had access to a professional coach who could guide my practice and give me feedback.

A teacher is a professional coach. Creating practice opportunities and being on hand to support students as they practise is an essential part of any teacher's job. From what they observe, they can give feedback, which informs practice. This **practice–feedback loop** is essential to propel learning forward:

---

124 https://educationendowmentfoundation.org.uk/evidence-summaries/teaching-learning-toolkit#closeSignup

Practice   Feedback

Like every other aspect of our teaching, **the purpose of the practice–feedback loop is to develop long-term memory.**

Feedback opportunities

At the risk of stating the obvious, to be able to give feedback to students, there has to be something to give feedback on. Students have to 'do something'. Lessons as lectures do not lend themselves to feedback. Neither does any activity that fails to produce *evidence of learning.*

> **Power-up Prompt 1:** Activities in lessons *generate evidence* to give feedback on.

Negative feedback

The fact that feedback can help learning should come as little surprise. It would actually be more surprising if research told us feedback *didn't* impact on learning positively. Well, prepare to be surprised! Research suggests that there *are* times when feedback can have a negative impact on learning.[125]

The right amount

One of these times is when we give students *too much* feedback. Despite what some people believe, more feedback does not necessarily mean more learning. Just as we can overwater plants, we can 'over-feedback' students. Giving them too much in too short a period of time will

---

125 Hendrick, C. and Macpherson, R. (2017) *What Does This Look Like in the Classroom?*

overload their working memory and, metaphorically, drown them. **Feedback needs to be chunked**. Little and often isn't a bad rule of thumb.

> **Power-up Prompt 2:** Feedback is delivered in *manageable chunks*.

Useful

Other times when feedback can have a negative impact on learning is when it isn't **useful**.[126] Useful feedback is that which students:

1. Understand
2. Know how to act on.

If feedback isn't perceived as useful, it can demotivate students. Hence, it impacts negatively on their learning.

'Accurate' doesn't necessarily mean 'useful'

A common misconception that teachers and school leaders have is that 'useful' means 'accurate'. However, that's not necessarily true.[127]

To appreciate this, consider the student who is given feedback that says, 'You need to improve your use of semi-colons.' This might be *accurate*, but if the student doesn't know how to do this, it's not particularly *useful*. If they knew how to do that, they probably would have done it already.

Current state vs goal state

Related to this point are the concepts of **'current state'** and **'goal state'**.[128] If feedback is to be useful to students, it needs to make clear *where they are* (current state), *where they need to be* (goal state), and *how to get there*:

---

126 Wiliam, D. (2011) *Embedded Formative Assessment*

127 Christodoulou, D. (2016) *Making Good Progress?*

128 Wiliam, D. (2011) *Embedded Formative Assessment*

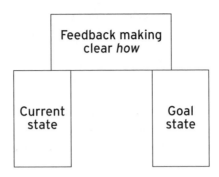

The importance of specificity

Specificity is an important principle when it comes to making feedback relating to the current state and goal state clear. Although, as we shall see shortly, specificity isn't enough in itself to make feedback useful, it is a necessary feature. Vague feedback is a sure-fire route to misunderstanding.

For example, if we are giving a student feedback to improve their front crawl in swimming, telling them to 'improve your front crawl' isn't particularly specific and, therefore, isn't particularly useful. If, instead, the student is told to 'improve *your breathing* during front crawl', this is more specific and, therefore, more useful (certainly, it is *starting* to be).

The feedback could be made *even more* useful if it is made *even more* specific. For example, telling the student to 'improve *your breathing* during front crawl' could mean:

- They aren't breathing often *enough*.
- They are breathing *too often*.

Just because the teacher understands what was meant doesn't mean the student does. We need to be as specific as we can, to help avoid misunderstandings.

Power-up Prompt 3: Feedback is as *specific* as possible.

Deconstructing performance

To help us give specific feedback to students, we will often need to 'deconstruct' performance, to identify *specific components* to give feedback on.

For example, imagine a student has attempted the following problem:[129]

> Several conductivity experiments were carried out using the apparatus below:

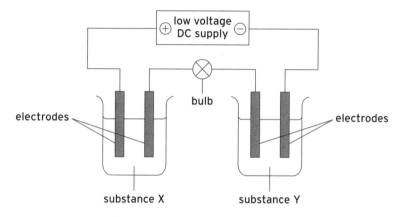

Identify the experiment in which the bulb would light.

	Substance X	Substance Y
A	Solid copper sulphate	Liquid mercury
B	Copper chloride solution	Molten sodium chloride
C	Solid potassium nitrate	Nickel bromide solution
D	Sodium chloride solution	Liquid hexane

The answer they give is 'A'. However, the correct answer is 'B'.

The problem is complex and can only be solved by integrating knowledge of different concepts. To give useful feedback, each concept needs to be isolated. Only by doing this can the teacher diagnose whether a student's

---

129 https://www.sqa.org.uk/pastpapers/papers/papers/2019/N5_Chemistry_all_2019.pdf

wrong answer was the result of misunderstandings in relation to one concept or another (or perhaps a combination of several).

Focus on *how*

As we have seen, specificity is important. However, if this specificity doesn't include *how* to move from the current state to the goal state, its usefulness will be limited, to say the least.

Returning to our front crawl example, if feedback has told a student that *they aren't breathing often enough*, the current state and the goal state are clear – the current state is they aren't taking enough breaths; the goal state is they need to breathe more often. But *how* do they get to the goal state? This isn't specified. It might be that they need to:

- Hold their breath for two seconds.
- Exhale slowly, using their mouth and nose.
- Pause for one second before taking a new breath.

It is detail of 'the how' that is most useful. Also useful would be to show them good examples of 'the how' in action.

Power-up Prompt 4: Feedback makes clear *how* performance can be improved.

Live feedback

Feedback doesn't need to be lengthy or written – it just has to be *useful*. Often, the most useful feedback is **Live Feedback (TT1)**. This is feedback that is given in *real time*, during interactions between teachers and students.

A student answers a question they are asked – they get *live feedback*. A teacher listens to what students are discussing – they get *live feedback*. A teacher looks at what students have written on **Show-me Boards (TT2)** or in their jotter – they get *live feedback*.

For example, imagine you are teaching students how to write the chemical symbols for ions. You have modelled this, and now you want students to practise the skill. You say: 'On your Show-me boards, write the chemical symbol for an aluminium ion.' You see the following:[130]

As students hold up their boards, you can give live feedback, which is *personalised to individuals*: 'Good', 'Good', 'Watch *that* – the "3" should come before the '+'.

Scanning

To do this well, you need to be good at **Scanning (TT3)**. This means taking in as much information as you can, from as many Show-me boards as you can, in as short a time as possible. Keeping students' responses on Show-me boards 'tight' should help with this.

For example, it shouldn't take much time to scan a set of 20 boards showing the chemical symbol for an aluminium ion. However, if you asked students to write the chemical symbol for a calcium ion and a potassium ion on their board as well, scanning would become much more difficult and time-consuming. You could scan one symbol three times much more quickly and efficiently than three different symbols once.

Whole-class feedback

Rather than give each student personalised feedback as you scan, instead, you might make a mental note of what you are seeing and give **Whole-class Feedback (TT4)** once you have finished looking at the boards.

For example, you might say:

- 'Okay, I saw that almost all of you have done *this* well. However, quite a few of you got *this* wrong. To avoid that, you need to make sure that you are doing *this*.'

---

130   What you should be seeing is: Al^{3+}.

- 'Remember: the success criteria I said I am looking for is *this*. *This* is what I want everyone to pay particular attention to. A good example is *this*.'

Whole-class feedback in this way can be just as useful to students as feedback that is personalised.

Use of Show-me boards creates the conditions for both. Through their use, *every* student can receive feedback on their performance.

Power-up Prompt 5: *Every student* receives feedback on their performance.

Written feedback

Some schools insist that teachers give written feedback, sometimes in jotters and sometimes in reports to parents. In inspections, a lack of evidence of written feedback can lead to poor ratings. Indeed, it is not uncommon to hear inspectors say things like, 'And we will be scrutinising jotters when we're in, making sure students are getting enough written feedback', as if because something appears in writing, it is better than something students have been told.

The belief that written feedback will be more useful to students than verbal feedback is delusion. Written feedback *can* be useful and there is a time and a place for it. However, more often than not, verbal feedback is better.

Feedback's usefulness should be evaluated in terms of the impact it has on moving students from their current state to a goal state – not by what form it takes.

A usefulness mirage

The learning gains that come from written feedback rarely warrant the time it takes teachers to write it. Too often, students don't understand what is written or don't know how to act on what is written. Messages that at first glance appear useful turn out not to be.

For example, consider the following written feedback:

- You used full stops very well, but you need to improve your use of commas.

- You are very good at calculating the circumference of a circle, but you have not yet mastered calculating the area. This is what I want you to focus on next.

- You have answered questions that require basic recall well, such as when you are asked to write definitions, but you aren't so good at explaining more complex concepts, such as why increasing temperature increases the rate of chemical reactions. This is the next step for you. To do this, I suggest that you spend more time revising the content of this topic.

The usefulness of such feedback is a mirage. By doing little more than *summing up learning*, comments of this kind are doing little more than a score or grade would. In effect, summative comments of this kind *are* scores and grades. The only real difference is that they take much more time to produce.

Better written comments?

A lack of specific detail about *how* to improve in the written comments we have considered means they aren't particularly *useful*. *How* do students improve their use of commas? *How* do they master calculating the area of a circle? *How* do they get better at explaining complex concepts? Students are left in the dark.

You could argue that the solution is for teachers to write better comments, by which we would mean giving more specific detail about how to improve. This would require more explanation and exemplification. But stop and think about this for a second. How long do you think it took teachers to write a class set of comments of the type we have already looked at? And now, we want them to write *more*?! *And*, we are assuming that students will understand what is written, which of course assumes that they will have read the comments in the first place. Being honest, some will have, but some won't. Paradoxically, writing *more* will actually lead to many students learning *less*. The reason is because the more they have to read, the less likely many will be to read them, and the less likely it is that many will be able to home in on what matters most.

Playing this out, let's assume that 80% of the class read your written comments and that 80% of those who read them understand what is written. Of these, 80% know how to act on this. In a class of 30 students, how many are we talking about? Fifteen. In other words, half the class. Now let's think about how long it took the teacher to write all of these comments. I think you can see where I am going with this. The time spent giving feedback in writing to individual students could be used far better.

Better verbal feedback

The best way to improve the feedback we give to students is **not to give more written feedback**. It's not even to improve what we write. Rather, it is to **concentrate on giving better *verbal feedback*.**

Rather than write comments in every jotter or at the end of every essay, teachers would be better reading student answers, making notes of common issues, and allocating time in class to discuss these with students, interactively. This is a smarter use of everyone's time. The value of marking is a delusion. Spending three hours a day marking jotters and writing feedback does not make you a better teacher. It will actually hold you back from improving, because you won't have any time to spend on activities that would be of more benefit to you and your students.

Giving verbal feedback, we can be sure a student has heard it, and we can do things to check it has been understood. Teachers need to concentrate on giving more verbal feedback during lessons. This means that they need to spend more time **planning activities that are good for generating evidence** on which feedback can be given.

Feedback records

If written **Feedback Records (TT5)** are required, students can maintain these themselves, based on what has been said to them by the teacher. By completing these, students will have to *think* about the feedback they have been given. **Students thinking about feedback is the single most important thing that must happen with it.** If feedback doesn't require thinking, then it is unlikely to lead to learning.[131] The accuracy of the Feedback Records students maintain should be a good indicator of how well feedback has been understood.

---

131   Wiliam, D. (2011) *Embedded Formative Assessment*

Active feedback

Feedback that students have to think about can be thought of as **'active feedback'**. The best way for feedback to become 'active' is to get students to 'do something with it' shortly after it has been given. 'Passive feedback' is feedback that students don't have to do anything with (but almost certainly should).

Have Another Go

Sometimes, active feedback will require students to **Have Another Go (TT6)**. The changes in performance that come from this will evidence the extent to which feedback has been understood.

Be a Detective

Other times, active feedback will involve the teacher saying something like:

- 'You got two of these right but one is wrong – I'd like you to work out which one is wrong, and why.'

- 'That's almost perfect, but I can see one mistake in what you've written. It's to do with the use of capital letters. See if you can find the mistake.'

In effect, the teacher is asking a student to **Be a Detective (TT7)**. They are pointing out that something is wrong and they are giving a clue as to what, but they aren't doing all of the work for the student. The student has to think for themselves.

With this technique, I would offer one note of caution: there is a fine line between, on the one hand, getting students to think in a way that moves learning forward, and, on the other hand, frustrating students. Asking them to be a detective relies on knowing students well enough to know that they have enough knowledge to both identify and correct mistakes. If they don't have this, then they won't be able to act on feedback, no matter how hard they think. We don't want students thinking: 'My teacher never gives me any help. They don't care about me.' Therefore, we shouldn't leave students to act as detectives for too long without checking in on the progress they are making. Even Inspector Morse needed support![132]

---

132 Feel free to repeat this anecdote, and feel free to replace 'Inspector Morse' with your detective of choice – or Jessica Fletcher.

> **Power-up Prompt 6:** Students have to *think* about the feedback they receive.

Monitoring performance

Once given, we need to ensure students have sufficient time to *act on feedback*. As they do, we should *monitor performance.*

Some students will have interpreted your feedback as you meant them to, meaning their performance should improve as intended. However, some won't. Even though you did everything you could to make clear *what* needed to improve and *how*, some students will have misunderstood aspects of this. If we don't watch students act on feedback, we won't know who these students are and the specific aspects they have misunderstood.

For this reason, ensuring students are given time to act on feedback is as important as ensuring they receive it in the first place.[133] We can't allow the demands of 'getting through content' to stop this integral part of the practice–feedback loop from happening.

> **Power-up Prompt 7:** Students are given *enough time to act* on feedback, so we can check they understand it.

Summary

Element 10: Feedback	
Power-up Prompts	**Trusted Techniques**
1	Activities in lessons *generate evidence* to give feedback on.	
2	Feedback is delivered *in manageable chunks*.	
3	Feedback is as *specific* as possible.	

---

133   Wiliam, D. (2011) *Embedded Formative Assessment*

Element 10: Feedback	
Power-up Prompts	**Trusted Techniques**
4 Feedback makes clear *how* performance can be improved.	
5 *Every student* receives feedback on their performance.	Live Feedback (TT1) Show-me Boards (TT2) Scanning (TT3) Whole-class Feedback (TT4)
6 Students have to *think* about the feedback they receive.	Feedback Records (TT5) Have Another Go (TT6) Be a Detective (TT7)
7 Students are given *enough time to act* on feedback, so we can check they understand it.	

Element 11:
Plenary Review

We only have a limited amount of time with our students. With this in mind, a key consideration for all teachers should be the impact that *each lesson* has on student learning. As John Hattie suggests, we should think of ourselves as 'evaluators of impact'.[134]

If we are to evaluate the impact of each lesson meaningfully, there needs to be *evidence* about what has changed over the course of a lesson. Having found out earlier in the lesson what students already know or can do, we need to build time into the ends of lessons to find out what they know or can do after something has been taught. As Hattie advises, 'the critical part when evaluating the lesson(s) is a review of the learning intentions and success criteria'.[135] This is what a **plenary** should be used for.

The purpose of plenaries

Lesson plenaries have two purposes:

1. *Sum up*, with reference to the learning intention.
2. *Gather evidence*, informed by the success criteria.

Plenaries offer a valuable opportunity to make the main learning points of a lesson clear, for students to think again about specific content, and to gather evidence that informs future teaching.

Despite their importance, in my experience plenaries are typically the weakest part of a lesson. Often they are rushed and sometimes they

---

134   Hattie, J. (2012) *Visible Learning for Teachers*
135   ibid.

don't happen at all. This is usually because the teacher hasn't planned enough time for the plenary or doesn't think it is important. If they are to function as anything more than tokenistic add-ons, plenaries need to be carefully planned and require around three to five minutes.

> **Power-up Prompt 1:** There is *sufficient time* for a meaningful plenary.

Learning intention

One of the functions of a plenary is to remind students of what they were supposed to be learning. We want them to leave lessons being clear about this. We made this clear at the start of the lesson, but a lot has happened since then. Now, we want to pull all of this together and remind students what the purpose of the lesson was, in terms of *learning*. We can do that by revisiting the learning intention with them in the plenary.

> **Power-up Prompt 2:** Students are reminded what the *learning intention* was.

Success criteria and assessment

Having reminded students what the learning intention was, we should then use *success criteria* to evaluate the extent to which they have achieved this. To do that, we need to *assess* learning.

Confidence measures

Sometimes when I observe lessons, I see teachers asking students to evaluate their learning using *confidence measures*. For example:

- 'Did everyone understand everything today?'
- Thumbs-up/thumbs-down
- Green, amber, red.

While useful for getting an *impression* about how students *feel*, such measures are unreliable as *evidence* of learning. Research suggests that most students will be overconfident.[136] They will tell us that they understand, or give us a 'thumbs-up' or a 'green', but really they don't

---

136   Kirschner, P.A. and Hendrick, C. (2020) *How Learning Happens*

understand as well as they think they do.[137] Such measures don't provide a true reflection of what has been learned. Some students won't even think about it – they will just tell us what they think we want to hear.

Evidence measures

Rather than use confidence measures, we need *evidence measures* that require students to **Prove it (TT1)** against the success criteria of the lesson. Useful Prove it approaches include:

- Short response questions
- Empty Your Brain
- True or false
- Multiple-choice questions.

> **Power-up Prompt 3:** Assessment in the plenary is linked to *success criteria* for the lesson.

Long- and short-term learning

Plenaries aren't about gathering evidence of *long-term learning* – they can't do that because not enough time has passed. You'd be better off using a future Daily, Weekly or Monthly Review for this purpose. Rather, plenaries are about gathering evidence of *short-term learning*, in relation to the content of *that lesson*.

Evidence that students know or can do what was intended at the end of a lesson is useful to help us evaluate its success. However, this doesn't mean that the content won't need to be revisited – it will. As we know, *learning fades*.

Evidence that students don't know or can't do something is just as useful as evidence that shows they can. It helps the teacher to know what needs to happen next, which might be that they need to reteach material, that students need more practice, or that the class can move on to new content.

> **Power-up Prompt 4:** Evidence produced in the plenary *informs future teaching*.

---

137   Remember what I said about *Homeland* in Learning Lesson 6.

Evidence from everyone

Earlier in this book, I discussed the importance of treating the class as 'a unit'. However, an important caveat is that this doesn't mean success criteria should be evaluated *collaboratively* – this needs to be an *individual* activity.

To appreciate this, imagine you are teaching a lesson on the anatomy of the heart to a class of 30 students. This has the following success criterion: 'I can name the four chambers of the heart.'

You want *every student* to be able to name *all four* chambers. A plenary that goes as follows does not assess this:

Teacher: 'Okay, so one of our success criteria for today's lesson is to be able to name each of the four chambers of the heart. Guy, please name one.'

Guy: 'The right atrium.'

Teacher: 'Good. Penny, please name a different one.'

Penny: 'The left atrium.'

Teacher: 'Good. Can anyone name the last two?'

[Henry shouts out.]

Henry: 'The right ventricle and the left ventricle.'

Teacher: 'Well done. I can see we've all got that. See you tomorrow.'

This sort of plenary is quite common. However, it doesn't evaluate *every* student's learning. As such, it is very limited in how useful it is to help us evaluate the impact of our lessons.

If instead, the teacher had asked everyone to draw a labelled diagram of the heart on **Show-me Boards (TT2)**, *everyone* would have been actively engaged and there would have been evidence of *everyone's* learning, gathered very quickly.

Exit Tickets

Rather than use Show-me Boards, students could have drawn their diagrams on paper. The advantage is that teachers can collect these, to look at more carefully. This technique is called **Exit Tickets (TT3)**.[138]

An Exit Ticket involves students responding to a task on a piece of paper (often a Post-it note) and giving this to their teacher before they leave. Evidence from these is used to inform future teaching.

As well as gathering evidence of what has been learned, Exit Tickets can be used by students to ask questions about something they are unsure about, or to highlight an area they are finding difficult. Not all students are comfortable doing this in front of the class, or approaching the teacher directly, but they will do this through an Exit Ticket.

> **Power-up Prompt 5:** *Every student* produces evidence of their learning.

Summary

Element 11: Plenary Review	
Power-up Prompts	**Trusted Techniques**
1	There is *sufficient time* for a meaningful plenary.	
2	Students are reminded what the *learning intention* was.	
3	Assessment in the plenary is linked to *success criteria* for the lesson.	Prove it (TT1) Show-me Boards (TT2)
4	Evidence produced in the plenary *informs future teaching*.	Exit Tickets (TT3)
5	*Every student* produces evidence of their learning.	

---

138 Lemov, D. (2015) *Teach Like A Champion 2.0*

Element 12:
Expectations, Behaviour
& Relationships

Social environments

Classrooms are social environments. How they feel to be in, and what is achieved while in them, depends on human interactions. Every time the teacher says or does something, it affects both individual students and groups. Sometimes the effect is intended and sometimes it isn't, but there is always an effect.

This is a key difference between teaching a single student in one-to-one tuition and teaching a class of multiple students. It's like dropping a stone in a pond: the ripples are far-reaching.

The 'Student Behaviour' Curriculum

For some of the students we are teaching, exemplary behaviour will be natural. For many, it won't be. **Students need to be taught how to behave**. This is why Tom Bennett suggests that behaviour is effectively its own curriculum.[139] Teachers' mastery of this curriculum is as important as mastery of their subject.

Six areas of this 'student behaviour' curriculum are key:

1. Expectations
2. Rules

---

139   Bennett, T. (2020) *Running the Room*

3. Routines
4. Corrections and consequences
5. Praise and rewards
6. Relationships.

We shall explore each one.

Expectations

The classroom culture we should be aiming for is one of mutual respect and co-operation.[140] This won't come about naturally. Rather, it needs to be developed, step by step. Fundamental to this development are the **expectations** of the teacher. The higher these are, the more you will get from your students, and the better they are likely to behave.

Not all teachers appreciate this. Many will simply 'put up' with sub-standard behaviour, believing nothing more is possible. 'That's just the students we get in this school,' they say, shrugging. If that's their mindset, they shouldn't be surprised when that's what they get. Setting a low bar is one of the worst things we can do in schools. It's a self-fulfilling prophecy.

Every student; every class

Every student can be taught to behave. As can every class. This is proven time and time again when the same class is taught by different teachers, behaving perfectly with one but poorly with another. Where there is a consistent pattern of this kind, teachers who are experiencing poor student behaviour do need to question their approaches to behaviour management. More often than not, the main issue is expectations that are too low.

This was brought home to me recently when I had a conversation with a teacher who had been struggling with poor student behaviour, but who had cracked the problem. 'I suddenly realised my expectations weren't high enough,' he told me. 'I wasn't clear in my own mind what I expected. I had heard other people say, "You need to have high expectations," and I thought that I did because I believed that was right, but then I realised I didn't, because I wasn't clear what my expectations were. Now I am, and so are my students. Everything is so much better!'

---

140   Nuthall, G. (2007) *The Hidden Lives of Learners*

> **Power-up Prompt 1:** There are *high expectations* for standards of student behaviour.

Modelling standards

For students to learn to behave as we expect, it is imperative that we *model standards* to them. How we interact with our students will influence how they interact with us. Speak with a coarse tone to them and don't be surprised when you get the same back. A 'New Radicals Principle' applies: you get what you give.[141]

This principle applies to all aspects of classroom behaviour, not just to interactions. For example, how you set work out on your board models how you expect students to set out work in their jotter. How tidy your classroom is influences students' perceptions of what you expect from them. The attention that you pay to spelling, grammar and presentation influences the attention that students pay to theirs.

> **Power-up Prompt 2:** High standards are *modelled* in everything we do.

Assertiveness

Much of what we expect of students is communicated implicitly, through our body language and use of voice. It is important to appreciate this, because students can sense anxiety from a hundred paces. For some, this is the perfect cue to see how much they can get away with.

Confidence

The best way to prevent this happening is to display *confidence*: confidence that *you* are in charge and in command of everything you are doing. Key to this are the following techniques:

- Assertive Address
- Radar.

An **Assertive Address (TT1)** means *confident oration* and *body language* whenever you are speaking to students. Through your use of voice,

---

141 'You Get What You Give' is a 1998 song by the American band, New Radicals.

movement and positioning in the room, you convey your authority. You're not just running the room – you *own* the room. This is *your* classroom, and *this* is what is happening. You make eye contact with every student and you expect them to make eye contact with you. They don't have anything in their hands while you are talking – they give you their full attention.

Radar (TT2)[142] is concerned with the teacher scanning the room at every opportunity, including when they are presenting to the class and working with groups of students. Nothing gets past them. Students know that their teacher is constantly scanning, so they behave. It is the *certainty* that they will get caught that is the deterrent. If this is in doubt, students won't worry about it, and so will be more likely to misbehave.

Rules

Rules are necessary to ensure expectations are met. They set out what, specifically, is acceptable, and what is not.

For example, you might have a broad *expectation* for students to be polite and courteous. You need specific *rules* to ensure this happens. These might include students putting up their hand when they want to speak, and never interrupting anyone. You might have a broad *expectation* that jotter work should be set out neatly. Specific *rules* might include that the date is always written in the margin, and headings are underlined using a ruler.

Rules are essential to ensure calm and ordered learning environments. Their absence is a sure-fire route to chaos and disaffection. If you have ever tried to play any game when no one knows the rules, or players are allowed to break the rules, you will understand this. No one enjoys it.

Rules for rules
Rules need to be **clear, specific** and **situation-focused**.

To appreciate this, imagine the following scenarios:

1. Students arriving at the classroom
2. Students entering the classroom

---

142   Lemov, D. (2015) Teach Like a Champion *2.0*

3. The teacher addressing the class
4. A student wanting to ask a question
5. A student wanting to answer a question
6. Students leaving the room.

What is it that you expect to happen during each of these scenarios? What is allowed and what isn't? You need to be clear about this, so you can establish clear rules.

Let's take 'the teacher addressing the class' as an example. Is it okay if students are writing? Is it okay if they are looking out of the window? Is it okay if they have their head on the desk? You need to consider all of these scenarios and make a decision in your own mind. Once determined, these become your *expectations*. Once communicated, they become your *rules*. In this sense, **rules are the articulation of specific expectations**.

You can't assume students will 'just know' your rules. How could they? *You* need to tell them. *They* need to practise applying them. *You* need to give them feedback about this. Does this sound familiar? It should: it's *teaching*.

As we have said, behaviour needs to be taught. Like any other learning, changes in behaviour result from changes in long-term memory. Just as we shouldn't be surprised when learning intentions aren't achieved with vague success criteria, so we shouldn't be surprised when students don't behave with vague rules.

Power-up Prompt 3: There are *clear, specific rules* for student behaviour in the *specific situations* that require them.

Routines

Over time, use of rules helps establish **routines**. When a routine is established, specific behaviours 'just happen', because everyone knows that's what is to happen. Routines make everyone's life easier, because students don't constantly need reminding about what the rules are. They are as important for teachers as they are for students.

Strong Start

One of the most important routines to establish is what happens at the start of a lesson. Get a lesson off to a **Strong Start (TT3)**[143] and it's likely it will go well from there. A poor start will most likely lead to the opposite.

A Strong Start involves students *getting equipment out quickly* and *engaging quickly.* This might relate to a task or to giving full attention to the teacher. Either way, the important point is: *quickly.* There isn't enough time to fritter it away.

Full Attention

Full Attention (TT4) means students have eyes and ears on you, with nothing in their hands. You might have to wait a moment to get full attention, but that matters far less than the fact that you get it. Addressing students when you don't have full attention will inevitably lead to disaster. It's one of the most common mistakes teachers with behaviour management issues make.

The act of waiting for full attention conveys assertiveness. You expect it, and you won't teach without it. If you need to, give a signal to a student who is taking too long to give you their full attention. Rather than an impersonal cue such as 'I'm still waiting' or 'I can stand here all day – it doesn't matter to me!', pausing or saying someone's name can be more effective. Saying 'Scott' should be enough to stop Scott from doing what he's doing and to get him to give his attention to you. Often, eye contact can be enough.

Resist Reacting

Sometimes, students will do something to convey their displeasure that they are having to do what they're told. For example, Scott might say 'Sorry!' in a sarcastic tone. In such cases, **Resist Reacting (TT5)**. More often than not, reacting will lead to unnecessary escalation. You can pick it up with the student later, when the heat has gone out of things.

For example, you might ask Scott to stay behind for a few minutes at the end of the lesson, when you can make clear to him that you don't expect answering back. Assuming this is communicated respectfully and Scott

---

143   Lemov, D. (2015) *Teach Like a Champion 2.0*

is given a right of reply, more likely than not he will accept this and the behaviour won't be repeated again. He might even apologise.

> **Power-up Prompt 4:** *Routines* are used to help make the room run smoothly.

Corrections and consequences

As important as everyone being clear about the rules and routines of a classroom is everyone being clear about what will happen if these aren't followed. This will involve a combination of **corrections** and **consequences**.[144] Corrections are subtle prompts and reminders. Consequences are more serious than this.

Examples of each are given in the table below:

Corrections	Consequences
A non-verbal intervention, such as a 'look' or a hand gesture - **Non-verbal Gestures (TT6)**	Giving a warning
Use of a student's name - **Use Names (TT7)**	Asking a student to step out of the room for a moment
Asking a question to get a student's attention - **Ask a Question (TT8)**	Moving a student's seat
Stopping what you are saying and standing still, looking at the student whose attention you expect - **Silent Stare (TT9)**	Phoning or emailing home
Moving towards a student as you are speaking - **Strategic Positioning (TT10)**	Issuing a detention
Having a quiet, private word with a student - **Private Conversation (TT11)**	

---

144   Lemov, D. (2015) *Teach Like a Champion 2.0*

Ideally, we would never have to use corrections or consequences, because student behaviour would be perfect. But this is unrealistic. Not making use of them is foolish. No student ever acts perfectly all of the time. If we don't use corrections and consequences, the one certain thing is that standards of behaviour will slide.

The balance of corrections and consequences

Corrections should have more of a use in our lessons than consequences. If we find ourselves issuing consequences on a regular basis, there is an underlying systemic issue that needs to be addressed. Consequences will quickly lose their effect if they are over-used in this way. Their principal purpose is as a *deterrent*, to stop poor behaviour from happening in the first place. It is the knowledge that a consequence exists and could be used that is most powerful.

Corrections

Having established clear rules and routines, it should be possible to manage most behaviour, most of the time, using corrections. These tend to be most effective when they:

1. **Are as low-key as possible** – *avoid sledgehammers to crack nuts.*

2. **Are as positive as possible** – *strictness doesn't mean 'horrible'.*

3. **Are directed at specific individuals** – *don't correct the whole class when you don't have to.*

4. **Cause minimal disruption to the flow of a lesson** – *make it quick and keep it light.*

To explore this, imagine a scenario in which Peter and Karen are talking while the teacher is explaining something to the class. To correct this behaviour, the teacher stops and shouts: 'Will everyone please PAY ATTENTION to what I am saying?! I am getting SICK AND TIRED of having to CONSTANTLY remind everyone to STOP TALKING!'

This approach doesn't fit any of the four criteria we have identified.

Contrast this with the following alternatives:

- The teacher stops talking and stands still, looking at Peter and Karen. After a few seconds, Peter and Karen realise what is happening and stop talking. The teacher says, 'Thank you' and continues with their explanation.

- The teacher continues with their explanation but walks towards Peter and Karen as they do so. As they get closer, Peter and Karen realise what is happening and stop talking.
- The teacher asks Karen a question. She answers it and the teacher thanks her for her answer but also says, 'Make sure you're paying full attention, please, Karen.'

You can take your pick with which of the alternatives you go with, but they all serve as better corrections to poor behaviour than the example we explored first.

Consequences

When corrections have failed, we should consider consequences. However, as we have already said, we shouldn't jump to their use too quickly. A law of diminishing returns tends to apply to their impact. When perceived by students as unjustified, they often exacerbate issues unnecessarily.

For example, imagine you have a rule that students shouldn't shout out answers. If a student shouts out an answer, sending them out of the room would be a *consequence* rather than a correction – and an unnecessary one. It would an over-reaction. Instead, a more appropriate lower-level correction would suffice: 'Ian, don't shout out. Thanks.'

However, just because you have used a correction with Ian, it doesn't mean his behaviour will change. He might shout out an answer again two minutes later, at which point a *consequence*, such as a formal warning, would be more appropriate: 'Ian, that's the second time you've done that. That's a warning.'

Ian should be clear about what it means to get a warning, because you will have made this clear to the class when you became their teacher. If a student is given a warning and they do something wrong again, there *will* be a higher-level consequence – there is no doubt about that.

So let's imagine that Ian shouts out again a minute later. Or perhaps he does something else that goes against the rules – perhaps he starts to talk to another student while you are talking. You're not going to give Ian *another* warning. If you do, it just sends a message that you're going to put up with more and more. But you're not.

Instead, you move to whatever consequence you have decided is warranted. Perhaps Ian will be told that he is to stay behind at the end of the lesson, asked to step out of the room for a few minutes, given an exercise to complete at home, or given a detention. The nature of the consequence is less important than the fact that it is given. Other students will see this happen. They are quick to work out which teachers follow through with what they say, and which don't.

If students know that they can behave in any way they like without consequence, then that's exactly what will happen. Some will behave, because they choose to, and some won't, because they choose not to. Despite what some school leaders would have you believe, **behaviour is a choice**.

The importance of consistency

Ensuring consequences are applied consistently in a classroom is a fundamental principle of effective behaviour management. Students need to know that *if I do this, this* will happen. As Bill Rogers points out, **consistency is more important than severity**.[145] The surest way to demonstrate to students that your expectations aren't high is that you let the little things go, even if that's just from time to time. The sure-fire way to get them complaining 'That's not fair!' is if consequences are applied to one student but not to another for the same behaviour.

Bounce Back

If and when we have used corrections and consequences, it is important that we give students the opportunity to **Bounce Back (TT12)**. Rather than let them think that we hold a grudge or we continue to be annoyed at them – which many will – we do something to show that it's in the past and forgiven. This might be as simple as giving them a smile or going out of your way to recognise something positive that they have done.

External support

As far as possible, teachers need to manage the behaviour of students in their classes themselves. If they don't, a perception can develop among

---

145   Rogers, B. (2015) *Classroom Behaviour*

students that the teacher isn't in charge. A 'learned helplessness' can also develop, with the teacher calling on external support at the first sign of an issue. This doesn't tend to help anyone, because the teacher has become dependent on someone else.

That said, there are times when external support may be required. Examples would include when a student point blank refuses to follow any instructions, despite use of corrections and consequences, or when a student swears at a teacher. In these cases, there should be a clear system for another adult to be called or for the student to be sent to that adult.

Power-up Prompt 5: Misbehaviour is managed though *consistent, proportionate use of corrections and consequences.*

Praise and Rewards

In earlier sections of this book, we discussed the fact that praise doesn't motivate students to learn (success does). However, that doesn't mean that classrooms should be praise-free zones! While it might not motivate students to learn, praise can make them feel good, which is an important feature of any learning environment.

Authentic Praise

When we use praise, we want it to be **Authentic Praise (TT13).** Authenticity comes from *the words we use* and *the way we say them.* Students are quick to recognise when praise is tokenistic and hollow.

For example, we can say 'excellent', but if students think this is hyperbole, it won't come across as sincere. As a result, it won't mean much to them. Often, 'good' or 'nice answer' is better. If, when we say 'good', we do so in a way that suggests we *mean it,* this will be perceived as authentic. If it comes across as a throw-away comment – perhaps something we say almost every time any student gives any answer – then it won't. If you throw praise around like confetti, it quickly loses its effect.

In the worst examples, teachers give praise to student answers or work that doesn't deserve it. For example, a student gives an answer that is half correct, and the teacher says, 'Great!' just because the student has said *something*. Because of the detrimental impact this will have on learning, it can't be framed as anything other than poor teaching.

Rewards

Just as consequences are a more formal form of correction, rewards are a more formal form of praise. They include things such as phone calls home, postcards and certificates.

Most students love rewards! However, like praise, they quickly lose their value if we use them too often. They need to be *earned*. Earning a reward should take quite a bit more effort than earning praise.

The pitfall of bribes

A common mistake that teachers make with rewards is that they try to use them as *bribes*. When they do this, good behaviour becomes transactional, dependent on the reward. The teacher says, 'If you do *this*, then you will get *this*.' But the problem with such an approach is that the student is no longer doing something because it is an expectation of the teacher. They are doing it because they *get something* in return. In effect, the teacher's authority has been eroded. Other students see what is going on and think, 'Hang on a minute! I do that anyway, without a reward.' They perceive the reward the other student is getting as unfair, and quite rightly so. Even if we can't see the negative impact this has on others, trust that it is there.

The ability to earn a reward needs to be a *level playing field*. Anyone could win one, so long as they meet the criteria, which are the same for everyone.

Power-up Prompt 6: There is authentic use of *earned praise and rewards* for effort and high-quality work.

Relationships

Expectations, rules, corrections, consequences, praise and rewards are all key ingredients of an effective behaviour curriculum. The final essential ingredient is **relationships**.

Relationships come about as a result of three things:

- knowing students well
- trust
- respect.

Knowing students well

Knowing students well starts with **knowing students' names**. It is essential that students feel valued and that they are more than a number. Taking time to learn the name of every student they teach is an essential thing for all teachers to do.

It continues by **making time for every student**. In every class we teach, there is the potential for some students to go unnoticed. Think of them as 'hidden students'. These are the students who never speak up and do very little to draw attention to themselves. Instead, they just get on with things quietly and speak when they are spoken to. They might take everything that the teacher says in, but the teacher doesn't do much to get anything out of them. Instead, the more extroverted students are allowed to dominate.

This isn't right. In any class, the learning of every student is as important as the learning of every other student. We need to make time to interact with *every student*. This doesn't mean that we need to sit down and have a one-to-one conversation in every lesson. That isn't usually practical. It just means that there needs to be *an interaction of some sort*. This might come about by addressing students by name as they arrive at or leave your class, a smile or a 'that's good' at opportune points in the lesson, or inviting students to say something during direct-interactive instruction. The teacher is mindful of everyone in the class, making a mental note about who has spoken and who hasn't. No one is forgotten or omitted.

> **Power-up Prompt 7:** Time is made to interact with *every student*.

Trust

Relationships are impossible without trust. For students to trust their teacher, they need to believe that their teacher:

1. Knows what they are talking about and what they are doing
2. Cares about them, both in terms of their learning and their wellbeing

3. Will intervene to help when they need them to

4. Means what they say and will do what they say.

In all cases, actions speak louder than words.

Mistakes

For example, imagine a teacher tells students, 'Being wrong is okay! We welcome mistakes in this classroom. Mistakes are how we learn.' Students trust that the teacher means this. Now imagine that the class is going through the answers to an assessment together, which the teacher has marked. Knowing her class well, the teacher knows who made particular mistakes in particular questions. Deliberately, she says to a student whom she knows made a particular mistake, 'Tom, what's six times three?' Tom replies: 'Eighteen.' 'So why did you put 21?' asks the teacher, sarcastically.

Tom feels embarrassed. His mistake has been made public and he has been made an example of. The teacher had told Tom that mistakes are okay, but Tom now knows that clearly they aren't. This *might* mean that he takes more care in his work. It almost certainly means that he has lost some trust in his teacher.

Students are always going to make mistakes. Sometimes these will be to do with deep-rooted misconceptions. Other times, they will just be careless errors. We *do* need to make it clear to students when they have made mistakes – it would be irresponsible not to. However, we need to be careful how we do this. Saying, 'No – that's not right', is fine. However, it is **never** acceptable to humiliate a student for their mistakes, whatever the intention behind this. As Sir John Jones tells us: students will forget much of what we teach them, but they will never forget how we make them feel.[146]

> **Power-up Prompt 8:** *Mistakes* are pointed out supportively, and used formatively.

Respect

A teacher–student relationship isn't one of equals. It is different from relationships with colleagues. *You* are the teacher. *You* are in charge. *You*

---

146 Jones, J. (2009) *The Magic-Weaving Business*

are responsible for the conditions, the ethos and the quality of teaching. That is a lot of responsibility for anyone. Students need to appreciate this. That means that they need to listen to what you say and follow your instructions.

Warm–strict

The relationships balance we should be aiming for in schools is **warm–strict**.[147] We should be warm in our interactions and strict in our insistence that expectations are met. Some of the best teachers I know, who have some of the best teacher–student relationships I have seen, are also the strictest teachers I know.

For some, the word 'strict' has developed negative connotations. This is misguided. 'Strict' means insisting that rules and routines are followed, and that corrections and consequences are applied fairly. In plain language, it means we're more than happy to have a laugh, but we won't put up with any nonsense. There is nothing negative about that. In the interests of good order and a happy experience for everyone, 'strict' is essential.

Where teacher–student relationships can often go wrong is when the 'warm–strict' balance is wrong. In an attempt to show students that they care, some teachers establish class conditions that are too informal and too laid back. There is a lot of *warmth* from the teacher towards their students, but there isn't enough *strict*. Inevitably, this leads to problems, the biggest of which is that the learning suffers.

The reverse can also be true. Some teachers are *overly* strict and, although I'm sure they do care, this doesn't always come across to students. They lack warmth. This leads to a different set of problems that also have a detrimental effect on learning.

> **Power-up Prompt 9:** There is a strong *'warm–strict'* behaviour balance.

---

147   Lemov, D. (2015) *Teach Like A Champion 2.0*

Summary

Element 12: Expectations, Behaviour & Relationships	
Power-up Prompts	**Trusted Techniques**
1 There are *high expectations* for standards of student behaviour.	
2 High standards are *modelled* in everything we do.	
3 There are *clear, specific rules* for student behaviour in the *specific situations* that require them.	Assertive Address (TT1) Radar (TT2)
4 *Routines* are used to help make the room run smoothly.	Strong Start (TT3) Full Attention (TT4) Resist Reacting (TT5)
5 Misbehaviour is managed though *consistent, proportionate use of corrections and consequences.*	Non-verbal Gestures (TT6) Use Names (TT7) Ask a Question (TT8) Silent Stare (TT9) Strategic Positioning (TT10) Private Conversation (TT11) Bounce Back (TT12)
6 There is authentic use of *earned praise and rewards* for effort and high-quality work.	Authentic Praise (TT13)
7 Time is made to interact with *every student.*	
8 *Mistakes* are pointed out supportively, and used formatively.	
9 There is a strong *'warm-strict'* behaviour balance.	

PART 3:
POWER UP TOGETHER

Powered-up Planning

In this book, we have explored 12 **Elements** of great teaching, identifying 75 **Power-up Prompts** and close to 100 **Trusted Techniques**. On the face of it, this could seem overwhelming. How is anyone supposed to focus on all of that?!

The good news is: you don't have to. While there is always scope to improve every aspect of every teacher's practice, at any one time there is rarely a need to focus on more than one thing. Pick an element and identify the Power-up Prompts and Trusted Techniques that are most likely to help you improve this. Focus on these until you have made the improvement you are satisfied with. Then you can turn your attention to something else.

If we accept the improvement journey is never-ending, we should realise that there is no need to rush, because there is no point at which we will ever be finished improving. Over the course of a year, it is more important that we see *real improvement* in a small number of areas than that we see incremental improvement in many.

The importance of planning

Good planning is almost always the key to improvement. Teaching is no exception.

While it is possible to 'plan in your head', most plans tend to benefit from being *written down* in a structured way. Doing so helps to clarify thinking and stop us forgetting what we had planned to do. By having something concrete that we can keep coming back to, we can hold ourselves accountable to ourselves. If we don't write our plan down, we are less likely to do that.

Professional Learning Plans

In *The Teaching Delusion*, I suggested a **Professional Learning Plan** template designed to support everyone to improve their teaching. It covered three areas:

1. **What:** the *specific aspect* of teaching practice you want to focus on improving

2. **How:** the *actions* you plan to take to bring about improvement

3. **Review:** the date your plan will be *revisited and updated.*

Now I suggest we update this format to build in the Elements, Power-up Prompts and Trusted Techniques discussed in this book.

An example is illustrated:

PROFESSIONAL LEARNING PLAN		
NAME: Teacher A		
DATE: 13 August 2021		
WHAT?	**Element(s)**	Questioning
	Power-up Prompt(s)	• *Every student* should think about every question asked. • Through *careful listening*, teaching responds to students' answers to questions. • Students should listen to and learn from *each other's answers*.
	Trusted Technique(s)	Show-me Boards
HOW?	**Reading** – what will you read?	*The Teaching Delusion*, pp. x -x
	Observation – who will you observe?	Teacher B and Teacher C
	Feedback – who will you ask to observe you and give you feedback?	Teacher D
	Participate – details of groups you will join, workshops you will attend, people you will collaborate with	Workshop on effective questioning, 1 September 2021 Weekly collaborative lesson planning with Teacher B
	Share – how will you share your learning with others?	At departmental meetings By writing a blog about what I've learned
REVIEW	When will you update this plan? (best if this is at least every 10 weeks)	October 2021

Motivation

In *Drive*, Daniel Pink suggests there are three factors that determine people's motivation:[148]

1. **Autonomy** – the desire to be self-directed
2. **Mastery** – the desire to get better at what we do
3. **Purpose** – the desire to be part of sometime bigger than ourselves.

Professional Learning Planning taps into all three factors. By taking charge of their own plan, teachers are *autonomous*. By identifying a specific focus and specific actions, teachers are pursuing *mastery*. With everyone in a school doing this, there is a shared sense of *purpose*. We are – all of us – going to get better, together!

Collaborative professional learning

To support this last point, teachers should be encouraged to share their Professional Learning Plans with other teachers. If they know someone else is focusing on improving the same element of practice as they are, it would make sense for them to work together. If someone sees that a teacher is working on a particular element of practice that they feel they have made real progress with themselves, they might want to get in touch with them about this.

---

148   Pink, D.H. (2009) *Drive*

Powered-up Coaching

A key premise of this book is that the quality of feedback teachers receive about their teaching isn't good enough. Professionals giving feedback need to get better at giving it! Knowing what you are talking about is essential, but so too is having a 'feedback framework' that guides your approach. The framework I suggest is: **SURF**.

SURF

When discussing lessons with teachers and giving feedback as part of this, we need to SURF. When we do this, we ensure that feedback is:

1. **S**pecific – it focuses on specific pedagogy

2. **U**nderstood – we check that the teacher understands it

3. **R**esearch-informed – as opposed to being based on opinion or ideology

4. **F**ollowed up – teachers need to know that they are practising the right things, in the right way, by having regular opportunities to discuss progress being made.

Link feedback to planning

If teachers have a Professional Learning Plan, then people observing lessons can link their feedback to this. Having access to the plan before observing a lesson, they can home in on the particular element of practice the teacher is focusing on improving. This is not to say that feedback can't be given on anything else, but feedback linked to the plan should be the priority.

Ask teachers what they want

If teachers don't have a Professional Learning Plan, ask them what they would like feedback on. You could do this before observing the lesson, which can help to guide what you focus on, or afterwards. Don't just blunder in and give teachers feedback on *anything*. If they identify specific areas themselves, they are then far more likely to value your feedback and act on it.

A coach, not a judge

Observed lessons should be a *low-stakes* opportunity for *rich discussion* about pedagogy. It is the process of reflection that is most important. The person who observed a lesson should be supporting this reflection, acting as a coach, not a judge. Judges reach verdicts; coaches help people to improve.

Lesson observations are not about drawing conclusions – they are about **supporting professional learning**. They are *formative*. If a teacher doesn't come out of a meeting to discuss a lesson feeling that it was useful, then it hasn't been.

The Power-up Prompts in this book have been written to support coaching. They are designed to act as a focal point for discussion. For example, if a teacher has asked for feedback on their *relationships* with students, the coach might discuss the following Power-up Prompts with them:

> **Power-up Prompt 7:** Time is made to interact with *every student*.

> **Power-up Prompt 8:** *Mistakes* are pointed out supportively, and used formatively.

> **Power-up Prompt 9:** There is a strong *'warm–strict'* behaviour balance.

Good coaching questions to help do this include:

- Do you feel that was the case?
- How true do you think this was for that lesson?

- Do you think there were any issues with this?
- Could this be improved? How?

Through use of questions like this, teachers are being coached to arrive at their own conclusions. This is almost always more powerful than a teacher being *told something* by someone else. Yes, there is benefit in someone pointing things out that a teacher might not have been able to see themselves and offering an alternative perspective. However, a teacher *realising something themselves* will almost always be more powerful. A good coach is a person who helps this to happen. They help pennies to drop.

Feedback meetings

With this in mind, inviting teachers to a 'feedback meeting' after an observed lesson doesn't quite chime with the culture we are trying to develop. Inviting teachers to *meet and discuss the lesson*, or to *have a chat about the lesson*, is less formal, and is better. 'Let's meet up to chat about the lesson' is a far warmer expression than 'We will have a meeting to evaluate this lesson.' I know which of the two I'd be feeling more anxious about!

'Feedback'

Following this principle through, perhaps the word 'feedback' is wrong. Perhaps it puts too much emphasis on teachers being 'told' something – '*this* was good'; '*that* wasn't so good' – when really it's the **conversation, reflection, advice** and **suggestions** that are most important.

But then again, this is often the way with words. They don't always convey the exact things we mean them to convey. It's unlikely that people will ever start to talk about having 'conversation, reflection, advice and suggestions meetings' with teachers after observed lessons. 'Feedback' serves as a catch-all term. We just all need to be clear about we really mean by this: *coaching*.

Pre-lesson coaching

Coaches don't always need to *observe* lessons. Sometimes, their work with teachers is more appropriate in the planning stages.

For example, if a teacher is focusing on improving the wording of learning intentions or the design of spotlight assessment activities, the coach might not need to see this 'live' in the classroom. They can go through a coaching process, using Power-up Prompts, in the planning stages:

> **Power-up Prompt 1:** The learning intention relates to specific *learning*, not doing.

> **Power-up Prompt 2:** The learning intention is *clearly worded*.

The coaching questions would be similar to those we have already looked at; it's just that the tense would change from past to present. For example:

- Do you feel this is the case?
- How true do you think this is?
- Do you think there are any issues with this?
- Can this be improved? How?

Practice lessons

Coaches can also work with teachers in *practice lessons*. For example, in a practice environment, they might use role play. Personally, I despise role play, but not everyone has the same aversion. Many teachers enjoy it and will benefit from it. It's simply a case of finding out what works best for different people.

Collaborative coaching

When we think about lessons being observed, we tend to think about school leaders observing them. However, teachers will often make better coaches than do school leaders. The key requirements to be an effective coach have nothing to do with position in a school. They have everything to do with **knowing what you are talking about and being competent at coaching.**

With this in mind, teachers should be supported and encouraged to 'buddy up' and form coaching groups. School leaders need to make sure that they give teachers time to do this. Through collaborative coaching, teachers can learn with and from each other, accelerating improvement in everyone's classroom.

Power up Together

Through a focus on **Elements, Power-up Prompts, Trusted Techniques** and the **SURF** feedback framework, *everyone* can be a coach. Stop for a moment and think how empowering that is! Rather than the pool of school coaches being limited to the minority of staff in leadership positions, coaching becomes universal. Instead of the incremental improvement we see in so many schools today, limited by leadership, we will see collaborative transformation, liberated by coaching.

What could be more exciting? What could be more important? What are you waiting for?!

Power up your pedagogy!

Appendix 1: Summary of Elements, Power-up Prompts and Trusted Techniques

Element 1: Daily Review	
Power-up Prompts	**Trusted Techniques**
1 Lessons begin with a *review activity*, requiring *recall from long-term memory*.	Last Lesson (TT1) Empty Your Brain (TT2) Teacher-quizzing (TT3) Show-me Boards (TT4) Self-quizzing (TT5) Peer-quizzing (TT6)
2 There is an appropriate blend of *recent and less recent material*.	
3 *All students* are engaged, thinking about what they should be thinking about.	
4 *A proportionate amount of time* is used for review activities.	
5 Activities provide *formative information to students*.	Student Review Record (TT7)
6 Activities provide *formative information to the teacher*.	Teacher Review Record (TT8)
7 *Weekly and Monthly Review* are used to complement Daily Review.	

Element 2: Learning Intentions	
Power-up Prompts	**Trusted Techniques**
1 The learning intention relates to *specific learning, not doing.*	WALT (TT1) 'Know...', 'Understand...' or 'Be Able to...' (TT2) Pique Interest (TT3)
2 The learning intention is *clearly worded.*	Stripped-back Language (TT4)
3 The learning intention is *clearly communicated*, visually and verbally.	Breathing Space (TT5)
4 There is appropriate emphasis in learning intentions to *highlight 'learning hooks'.*	Signalling (TT6)
5 The learning intention is *specific to the lesson being taught.*	

Element 3: Success Criteria	
Power-up Prompts	**Trusted Techniques**
1 Success criteria *clearly communicate* what you are looking for.	'I Can...' Statements (TT1) Key Features (TT2) Exemplars (TT3)
2 Success criteria *are shared and revisited at appropriate points* in the lesson.	
3 Success criteria are specific enough so that *learning can be evaluated.*	Prove it (TT4)
4 *All students* prove their learning against *each* of the success criteria.	

Element 4: Prior Knowledge	
Power-up Prompt	Trusted Techniques
1 Assessment is used to *explore students' prior knowledge*, activating relevant schemata and guiding future teaching.	KWL Grid (TT1) Concept Cartoons (TT2) True or False (TT3) Odd One Out (TT4) Empty Your Brain (TT5) Deliberate Mistakes (TT6) Multiple Choice (TT7) Show-me Boards (TT8)

Element 5: Presenting Content	
Power-up Prompts	**Trusted Techniques**
1 *Presentations are interactive,* holding students' attention and making everyone think.	Cold Call (TT1) Chunk it (TT2) Varied Voice (TT3) Pause for Effect (TT4)
2 Resources and presentations are carefully designed to support students to *focus on the specific content* that we want them to be thinking about.	Signalling (TT5) Reveal Slowly (TT6) Breathing Space (TT7) Stripped-back Slides (TT8)
3 As far as possible, *visual representations* are blended with *complementary narration,* avoiding unnecessary written text.	Verbal Visuals (TT9) Integrated Text and Visuals (TT10)
4 Presentations include *multiple concrete examples and non-examples.*	
5 Steps are taken to make content *interesting.*	Present a Problem (TT11) Tell a Story (TT12)
6 Strategies are used to help students *memorise core content.*	Analogies (TT13) Mnemonics (TT14) Build in Retrieval (TT15) Rehearse in Your Head (TT16) Instruct Memorisation (TT17)
7 There are *frequent checks for understanding.*	Boomerang (TT18)
8 Where necessary, content in presented in *an alternative way.*	

Element 6: Practice	
Power-up Prompts	**Trusted Techniques**
1 Practice focuses on the improvement of *specific knowledge and skills.*	
2 Guided practice is used to *model success* and *gauge student understanding.*	Descriptive Modelling (TT1) Scaffolding (TT2) Split Screen (TT3) Show-me Boards (TT4) Live Feedback (TT5)
3 Guided practice examples are *carefully sequenced by difficulty,* avoiding cognitive leaps that are too big.	
4 Guided practice achieves an *80% success rate.*	
5 As required, *supported practice* is used to consolidate learning from guided practice.	Circulate the Room (TT6) Hushed Voice (TT7)
6 Students are given the opportunity to practise *independently.*	
7 *Spaced practice* is built into the practice sequence.	Repeated Revisits (TT8)
8 *Interleaved practice* is built into a practice sequence at an appropriate point.	Interleaving (TT9)
9 Practice opportunities require students to *think about content in multiple ways.*	Different Angles (TT10)
10 Students have access to resources that allow them to *evaluate their own learning.*	Self-assessment (TT11)
11 Students have access to *timely support* as they are practising.	Peer-assessment (TT12)

Element 7: Differentiation	
Power-up Prompts	**Trusted Techniques**
1	*The 80% Rule* is used to guide decisions about what to do next.	
2	Every student has *access to support*, as and when they need it.	Peer Teaching (TT1) On-hand Help (TT2) Temporary Grouping (TT3)
3	Activities create *desirable difficulties*, getting all students to *think hard*.	Three-metre Ditches (TT4) Guard Against Guessing (TT5) Confidence Measures (TT6)
4	There is a *common core*, with *overlearning opportunities* that go beyond this.	
5	*Choices within activities* offer appropriate support and challenge to everyone, but keep the class as close together as possible.	Chilli Pepper Challenge (TT7) Pick & Mix (TT8) Guide Choice (TT9)
6	Students who have *mastered content* are used as a teaching resource for others.	Create Your Own (TT10) Become the Teacher (TT11)

Element 8: Questioning	
Power-up Prompts	**Trusted Techniques**
1 Teacher exposition is infused with *frequent questioning*.	
2 Students have *sufficient background knowledge* to answer the questions we ask.	
3 *Every student* is expected to think about *every question* asked.	Show-me Boards (TT1) Cold Call (TT2) Pause (TT3) Bounce (TT4) Catch (TT5) On the Hook (TT6)
4 Questioning is used to explore both *surface knowledge* and *deep understanding*.	Drill Down (TT7)
5 Through *careful listening*, teaching engages with students' answers, including the *specific detail* of these.	Homing in (TT8)
6 Students listen to and learn from *each other's answers*.	Say it Again, Louder (TT9) Amplify (TT10)
7 Students who can't answer questions are *supported and challenged* to learn what they need to answer these in future.	I'll Come Back to You (TT11) Phone a Friend (TT12)

Element 9: Discussion	
Power-up Prompts	**Trusted Techniques**
1 Students have sufficient *background knowledge* to participate in discussions.	
2 Discussions are *focused on specific learning.*	
3 Discussions are managed so *all students* participate and learn from each other.	Invite Them in (TT1) Controlled Turns (TT2) Chat to a Partner (TT3)
4 Key points that emerge from discussions are *emphasised* and *made clear.*	Say it Again, Louder (TT4) Amplify (TT5) Polished-up Points (TT6) Chart it (TT7)
5 There is due care to *avoid teaching biases or allowing offence to be caused.*	

Element 10: Feedback	
Power-up Prompts	**Trusted Techniques**
1 Activities in lessons *generate evidence* to give feedback on.	
2 Feedback is delivered in *manageable chunks.*	
3 Feedback is as *specific* as possible.	
4 Feedback makes clear *how* performance can be improved.	
5 *Every student* receives feedback on their performance.	Live Feedback (TT1) Show-me Boards (TT2) Scanning (TT3) Whole-class Feedback (TT4)
6 Students have to *think* about the feedback they receive.	Feedback Records (TT5) Have Another Go (TT6) Be a Detective (TT7)
7 Students are given *enough time to act* on feedback, so we can check they understand it.	

Element 11: Plenary Review	
Power-up Prompts	**Trusted Techniques**
1 There is *sufficient time* for a meaningful plenary.	
2 Students are reminded what the *learning intention* was.	
3 Assessment in the plenary is linked to *success criteria* for the lesson.	Prove it (TT1) Show-me Boards (TT2)
4 Evidence produced in the plenary *informs future teaching.*	Exit Tickets (TT3)
5 *Every student* produces evidence of their learning.	

Element 12: Expectations, Behaviour & Relationships	
Power-up Prompts	**Trusted Techniques**
1 There are *high expectations* for standards of student behaviour.	
2 High standards are *modelled* in everything we do.	
3 There are *clear, specific rules* for student behaviour in the *specific situations* that require them.	Assertive Address (TT1) Radar (TT2)
4 *Routines* are used to help make the room run smoothly.	Strong Start (TT3) Full Attention (TT4) Resist Reacting (TT5)
5 Misbehaviour is managed though *consistent, proportionate use of corrections and consequences.*	Non-verbal Gestures (TT6) Use Names (TT7) Ask a Question (TT8) Silent Stare (TT9) Strategic Positioning (TT10) Private Conversation (TT11) Bounce Back (TT12)
6 There is authentic use of *earned praise and rewards* for effort and high-quality work.	Authentic Praise (TT13)
7 Time is made to interact with *every student.*	
8 *Mistakes* are pointed out supportively, and used formatively.	
9 There is a strong *'warm-strict'* behaviour balance.	

Appendix 2:
Summary of Key Effects and Principles

The Coherence Principle	Minimise unnecessary words and pictures when presenting content. Keep it as simple as possible. Being more accurate by saying more will often get in the way of students learning what we want them to learn. Cut out the chunks of text and fancy clip-art. This will reduce cognitive load.
The Expertise Reversal Effect	Pedagogy that is highly effective for 'novices' - such as direct-interactive instruction - can lose its effectiveness when used with 'experts'. Experts will often benefit from pedagogy that is less teacher-led. Pedagogy that can be effective for experts - such as student-led approaches - is unlikely to be effective for teaching novices.
The Interleaving Effect	When we 'interleave', we mix up what we are practising. Rather than attempt the same type of problem one after the other, we intersperse different types of problems, in a random way. The effort associated with jumping from one thought process to another helps strengthen learning.
The Hypercorrection Effect	The shock associated with giving an answer to a question we are sure is correct, but then find out is wrong, strengthens the memory of the correct answer.

The Modality Effect	Modality relates to the form in which content is presented. For example: written words, spoken words, or images.
	Written words and *spoken words* exist in the same modality and are processed by working memory in the same way. The same is true for *written words* and *images*. Presenting written words and spoken words together, or written words and images together, has a cumulative effect on cognitive load.
	However, *spoken words* and *images* exist in different modalities and are processed differently in working memory. Rather than their effects being cumulative, they are *complementary*.
	Cognitive load should be lowest if content is presented using complementary modalities, rather than cumulative ones.
The Redundancy Effect	When the *same information* is communicated in *written* and *spoken* forms *at the same time*, one of the forms is redundant. Rather than have a neutral effect, this actually affects learning negatively. Trying to 'filter out' the redundant form causes unnecessary cognitive load. Avoid reading out too much text on your PowerPoint slides.
The Self-Explanation Effect	Students' stopping and thinking to themselves, 'I wonder what that means?', 'Why is that?', 'If that's the case, is this the case as well?', are examples of self-explanation. Where this happens, students are having internal conversations with themselves, trying to make sense of things. Through its effect on schemata development, this can have a very positive impact on learning.
The Signalling Principle	Learning is most likely to happen when a deliberate attempt is made to think about specific things. If we use signals such as bold text, underlining, colour, and arrows, we can focus attention and thought on specific information.

The Spacing Effect	We learn better when *multiple exposures* to the *same content* are *spaced out*, rather than back to back. The act of starting to forget something, and the effort that is then required to retrieve the memory of this, has a positive impact on learning.
The Split-Attention Effect	If students are required to get information from more than one place in order to make sense of it, then we are splitting attention and causing unnecessary cognitive load. If students are working on a task we have set them, we should avoid talking to them while they do this, for example, by saying 'Remember to...' or 'Make sure that you...'. If they are looking at a diagram that requires text to understand it, this should be integrated with the diagram, rather than somewhere separate.
The Testing Effect	The act of retrieving knowledge from long-term memory strengthens the memory of it.
The Transient Information Effect	Verbal information is transient because, as soon as it is said, it 'disappears'. The only way to hold onto it is using working memory or long-term memory. This isn't a problem if the amount of transient information is tightly controlled, but it *is* problem if there is too much of it. This will lead to significant cognitive load. The way to minimise this load is to ensure key words and phrases, including those that students will need to refer back to, are written down for students to see. This is especially important when these are unfamiliar.

References

Ausubel, D., Novak, J. and Hanesian, H. (1978) *Educational Psychology: A Cognitive View* (2nd edition). New York, NY: Holt, Rinehart & Winston.

Barton, C. (2018) *How I Wish I'd Taught Maths: Lessons Learned from Research, Conversations with Experts, and 12 Years of Mistakes.* Woodbridge: John Catt Educational Ltd.

Bennett, T. (2020) *Running the Room: The Teacher's Guide to Behaviour.* Woodbridge: John Catt Educational Ltd.

Bjork, E.L. and Bjork, R.A. (2014) 'Making Things Hard on Yourself, But in a Good Way: Creating Desirable Difficulties to Enhance Learning'. In Gernsbacher, M.A. and Pomerantz, J. (eds) *Psychology and The Real World: Essays Illustrating Fundamental Contributions to Society* (2nd edition). New York, NY: Worth, pp. 59–68.

Butterfield, B. and Metcalfe, J. (2006) 'The Correction of Errors Committed with High Confidence', *Metacognition and Learning*, 1(1), pp. 69–84.

Caviglioli, O. (2019) *Dual Coding with Teachers.* Woodbridge: John Catt Educational Ltd.

Christodoulou, D. (2016) *Making Good Progress?: The Future of Assessment for Learning.* Oxford: Oxford University Press.

Clarke, S. (2014) *Outstanding Formative Assessment: Culture and Practice.* London: Hodder Education.

Coe, R., Rauch, C.J., Kime, S. and Singleton, D. (2019) *Great Teaching Toolkit: Evidence Review.* Evidence Based Education.

Enser, M. (2019) 'Education Myths: An Origin Story', in Barton, C. (ed.) *The researchED Guide to Education Myths*. Woodbridge: John Catt Educational Ltd, pp. 19–27.

Harari, Y.N. (2015) *Sapiens*. London: Vintage.

Hattie, J. (2012) *Visible Learning for Teachers: Maximizing Impact on Learning*. New York, NY: Routledge.

Hendrick, C. and Macpherson, R. (2017) *What Does This Look Like in the Classroom? Bridging the Gap Between Research and Practice*. Woodbridge: John Catt Educational Ltd.

Jones, J. (2009) *The Magic-Weaving Business: Finding the Heart of Learning and Teaching*. London: Leannta Publishing.

Kirschner, P.A. and Hendrick, C. (2020) *How Learning Happens: Seminal Works in Educational Psychology and What They Mean in Practice*. Oxon: Routledge.

Kirschner, P.A., Sweller, J. and Clark, R.E. (2010) 'Why Minimal Guidance During Instruction Does Not Work: An Analysis of the Failure of Constructivist, Discovery, Problem-based, Experiential, and Inquiry-based Teaching', *Educational Psychologist*, 46(2), pp. 75–86.

Lemov, D. (2015) *Teach Like a Champion 2.0: 62 Techniques that Put Students on the Path to College*. San Francisco, CA: Jossey-Bass.

Lovell, O. (2020) *Sweller's Cognitive Load Theory in Action*. Woodbridge: John Catt Educational Ltd.

Mayer, R.E. (2008) 'Applying the Science of Learning: Evidence-based Principles for Designing Multimedia Instruction', *American Psychologist*, 63(8), pp. 760–769.

Mayer, R.E. (2020) *Multimedia Learning* (3rd edition). Cambridge: Cambridge University Press.

McCourt, M. (2019) *Teaching for Mastery*. Woodbridge: John Catt Educational Ltd.

Mccrea, P. (2017) *Memorable Teaching: Leveraging Memory to Build Deep and Durable Learning in the Classroom.* CreateSpace Independent Publishing Platform.

Myatt, M. (2018) *The Curriculum: Gallimaufry to Coherence.* Woodbridge: John Catt Educational Ltd.

Naylor, S. and Keogh, B. (2000) *Concept Cartoons in Science Education.* Cheshire: Millgate House Publishers.

Naylor, S., Keogh, B. and Goldsworthy, A. (2004) *Active Assessment in Science: Thinking, Learning and Assessment in Science.* London: David Fulton.

Nuthall, G. (2007) *The Hidden Lives of Learners.* Wellington: Nzcer Press.

Pink, D.H. (2009) *Drive: The Surprising Truth About What Motivates Us.* New York, NY: Riverhead Books.

Robertson, B. (2020) *The Teaching Delusion: Why Teaching in Our Schools Isn't Good Enough (And How We Can Make It Better).* Woodbridge: John Catt Educational Ltd.

Robertson, B. (2021) *The Teaching Delusion 2: Teaching Strikes Back.* Woodbridge: John Catt Educational Ltd.

Rogers, B. (2015) *Classroom Behaviour: A Practical Guide to Effective Teaching, Behaviour Management and Colleague Support.* London: SAGE Publications Ltd.

Rosenshine, B. (2012) 'Principles of Instruction: Research-Based Strategies That All Teachers Should Know', *American Educator,* 36(1), pp. 12–19.

Sherrington, T. (2017) *The Learning Rainforest: Great Teaching in Real Classrooms.* Woodbridge: John Catt Educational Ltd.

Sweller, J. (1988) 'Cognitive Load During Problem Solving: Effects on Learning', *Cognitive Science,* 12, pp. 257–285.

Thom, J. (2020) *A Quiet Education: Challenging the Extrovert Ideal in Our Schools.* Woodbridge: John Catt Educational Ltd.

Weinstein, Y. and Sumeracki, M. (2019) *Understanding How We Learn: A Visual Guide*. London: Routledge.

Wiliam, D. and Leahy, S. (2015) *Embedding Formative Assessment*. West Palms Beach, FL: Learning Sciences International.

Wiliam, D. (2011) *Embedded Formative Assessment*. Bloomington, IN: Solution Tree Press.

Wiliam, D. (2018) *Creating the Schools Our Children Need: Why What We're Doing Now Won't Help Much (And What We Can Do Instead)*. West Palms Beach, FL: Learning Sciences International.

Willingham, D.T. (2009) *Why Don't Students Like School? A Cognitive Scientist Answers Questions About How the Mind Works and What It Means for the Classroom*. San Francisco, CA: Jossey-Bass.

Zeffman, H., Smyth, C. and Swinford, S. (2021) 'Mass testing blitz as Boris Johnson plans easing of lockdown', *The Times*, 17 February.

Acknowledgements

The Teaching Delusion 3 is a book that was never meant to be! It emerged out of the writing process for *The Teaching Delusion 2*, when it dawned on me that I had written two very different books. For the Tom Waits fans out there, *The Teaching Delusion 3* is the 'Alice' to *The Teaching Delusion 2*'s 'Blood Money'. For Nick Cave and the Bad Seeds fans, it's 'The Lyre of Orpheus' to *The Teaching Delusion 2*'s 'Abattoir Blues'. For those into the Pet Shop Boys, it's the 'Relentless' to *The Teaching Delusion 2*'s 'Very'. For anyone who's no idea what I'm talking about, I'll stop there!

Although somewhat of an accidental book, I'm delighted that *The Teaching Delusion 3* has come to be. It completes *The Teaching Delusion* trilogy and is the book that my husband, Jamie, has always encouraged me to write: a straightforward, no-nonsense user's guide to classroom practice.

Over the course of the three years it has taken to write *The Teaching Delusion* trilogy, I have had a wonderful team supporting me. These include my husband, Jamie, friends who have read early drafts – with a particular mention to Derek Huffman and Ian Yule – and my parents, who have always been a tremendous support. Sadly, my dad passed away during the writing of this book. I'm fairly certain he'd never have read it, but I'm equally certain he'd have been very proud that it was written. *The Teaching Delusion 3* is dedicated to him.

There are a number of other people I'd like to acknowledge and thank for their contribution to this book. These include Kate Jones, who has written a wonderful foreword, Tom Sherrington, Carl Hendrick, Jamie Thom, Zoe Enser, Michael Chiles, Fiona Leadbeater, Colin McGill and

Colin Richardson, for reading advance copies and writing 'Praise For' quotes, Gráinne Treanor, my brilliant proofreader, and Alex Sharratt, Jonathan Barnes and everyone else at the John Catt Educational team. Their support has been incredible.

Finally, I would like to thank everyone who has helped promote *The Teaching Delusion* trilogy and taken the time to get in touch with me about it. I've been blown away by the reception to the first book and am delighted that so many people across the world have found it so useful. I hope this book is just as useful.

Teaching is the most important and rewarding job in the world. If *The Teaching Delusion* trilogy has helped to make just one teacher's teaching better, then it has done its job. If it has helped you, I'd love to hear from you. Please get in touch!

Bruce Robertson

August 2021

Also available in this series

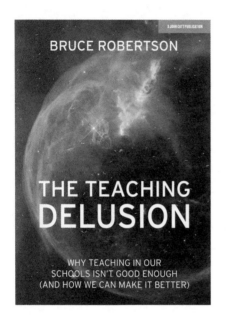